GREAT RUNNING BACKS OF THE NFL

The colorful stories of eleven of the NFL's most famous and successful running backs. They are Jimmy Brown, Paul Hornung, Jim Taylor, Gale Sayers, Red Grange, Bronko Nagurski, Ollie Matson, Hugh McElhenny, Joe Perry, Steve Van Buren and Ernie Nevers.

GREAT RUNNING BACKS OF THE NFL

BY JACK HAND

illustrated with photographs

RANDOM HOUSE • NEW YORK

GREAT RUNNING BACKS OF THE NFL by Jack Hand

Photograph credits: Bettmann Archives, page 39; J. Vernon Biever, pages 14, 59, 67, 109, 116-117, 123, 124, 139, 170-171; Malcolm Emmons, pages 5, 8, 11, 19; Ken Regan, pages 70-71, 163; United Press International, pages 23, 26-27, 30-31, 44-45, 53, 61, 87, 88-89, 97, 102 (bottom), 120-121, 129 (top), 133, 136-137, 141, 147, 157, 158-159, 167, 173, 176-177; Wide World, pages 17, 32-33, 46-47, 64-65, 77, 79, 95, 102-103 (top), 105, 114, 129 (bottom), 154.

Library of Congress Catalog Card Number: 66-10694

Manufactured in the United States of America

Designed by Jackie Corner

CONTENTS

Introduction

In writing this book about great running backs, selecting the men who should be covered presented a most difficult problem. The author considered concentrating on heroes of the days before the forward pass when running backs won all the battles and grabbed all the headlines. He also considered glossing over the past to concentrate on current stars.

With some misgivings, it was decided to mix the old with the new, taking some stars from each period. Obviously, it has been necessary to leave many fine running backs out. It was not possible to make the list all-inclusive. Regrettably, some fans may find their favorites missing.

Red Grange, Ernie Nevers, and Bronko Nagurksi have been chosen to represent the distant past. Steve Van Buren, Joe Perry, Hugh McElhenny and Ollie Matson represent the more recent past. As for the present, Jim Brown was a must and Paul Hornung and Jim Taylor could not be overlooked. Gale Sayers' remarkable feats as a rookie in 1965 made him the logical choice to represent the future as well as the present.

Many other great runners could have been included. Frank Gifford and Lenny Moore have already been covered in Heroes of the NFL (Punt, Pass and Kick Library #4). Other present-day stars who might have been included are Jon Arnett, J. D. Smith, John Henry Johnson, Tommy Mason, Nick Pietrosante, John David Crow, Dick Bass, Don Perkins, Bill Brown, Tim Brown, Ken Willard and Tucker Frederickson.

Some of the great runners of the past who could not be included are George McAfee, Cliff Battles, Beattie Feathers, Deacon Dan Towler, Tony Canadeo, Bill Dudley, Ace Gutowsky, Dutch Clark, Doak Walker, Marion Motley, Frank Filchock, Pat Harder, Alan Ameche, Clarke Hinkle, Tank Younger, Bill Osmanski, Elmer Angsman, Dub Jones, Tuffy Leemans, Ed Price, Bill Paschal, Andy Farkas, Willie Galimore, Charlie Trippi, Bob Hoernschemeyer, Alex Webster and Rick Casares.

With apologies to those who could not be covered and with thanks to those who were so helpful in gathering material, we present the book for your enjoyment.

Jack Hand

GREAT
RUNNING BACKS
OF THE NFL

JIM
BROWN
chapter
one

In the mid-1950s the football team at the University of Syracuse had begun to move toward top national ratings under coach Ben Schwartzwalder. Colgate, Syracuse's neighbor and traditional rival, on the other hand, had veered away from big-time football. It was becoming clear that the two teams could not continue their football rivalry on even terms.

The final proof came in 1956. The Syracuse-Colgate game was the last of the season for both teams. Syracuse was hoping to attract an invitation to a major bowl game and needed a rousing victory. Colgate, outmanned but eager, was ready for the challenge.

Before Colgate finally dragged itself off the field on the short end of a 67-6 score, a Syracuse senior named Jim Brown had scored a staggering total of 43 points, setting a major college record. He had scored six touchdowns, kicked seven conversions and gained 197 yards. Syracuse got its invitation to play Texas Christian University in the Cotton Bowl. Jim Brown was chosen to most All-America teams. He would soon go on to greater glory in the National Football League.

James Nathaniel Brown was born February 17, 1936, at St. Simon Island, Georgia. When he was two his parents separated, and his mother moved to Manhasset, New York. For a time Jim stayed behind with his grandmother in Georgia, but five years later he joined his mother in the North.

As a teenager Jim had a brilliant athletic career at Manhasset. High School. Forty-five colleges offered him scholarships, but he decided to attend Syracuse, where a scholarship depended on his performance as a freshman.

Jim Brown relaxes on the sidelines.

Jim's accomplishments during his freshman year were not remarkable, and by June he was nearly ready to quit. But he stuck with it and made the varsity football team as a sophomore. From then on, he had one success after another. By the time he was graduated, he had gained 2,091 yards, scored 187 points and tallied 25 touchdowns. After scoring 43 points against Colgate in the 1956 game, he led Syracuse to the Cotton Bowl against Texas Christian. There he scored 21 points, but Syracuse lost by a heartbreaking 28-27.

Brown was and is a tremendous all-around athlete. When he was in college, the New York Yankees were interested in his baseball skills. Although the football season, with its bowl games, ran into January and resumed with spring practice in April, Jim found time to play 43 basketball games on the Syracuse varsity and scored 563 points.

Next to football, track and lacrosse were Brown's best sports at Syracuse. He made All-America in lacrosse. He once said that he would like to play lacrosse five days a week and football on Saturday. In track, while just a sophomore, he placed fifth in the national decathlon championships.

Roy Simmons, the Syracuse boxing coach, once said he could have made Jim the intercollegiate boxing champion if he had come out for the sport. Norman Rothschild, a Syracuse boxing promoter, offered Jim $25,000 to become a professional heavyweight. In 1960 Rothschild increased his offer to $100,000.

In his last day as a Syracuse sports hero, Jim shuttled between a morning track meet and an afternoon lacrosse game. In the track meet, he won the high jump and the discus and placed second in the javelin to score 13 points. Syracuse won, 72-59. Then he led the Syracuse lacrosse team to an 8-6 victory over Army.

Despite his excellence in other sports, Jim's big game remained football. Offers poured in from baseball teams, boxing promoters and others, but the offer that really counted was the one from the Cleveland Browns in the National Football League. The Browns picked Jim in the first round of the college draft. After playing briefly for the College All-Stars in the 1957 All-Star Game, Jim reported directly to the Browns' training camp.

Jim got his first trial in the Browns' first exhibition game against the Pittsburgh Steelers. He took the ball on a draw play and broke loose for a

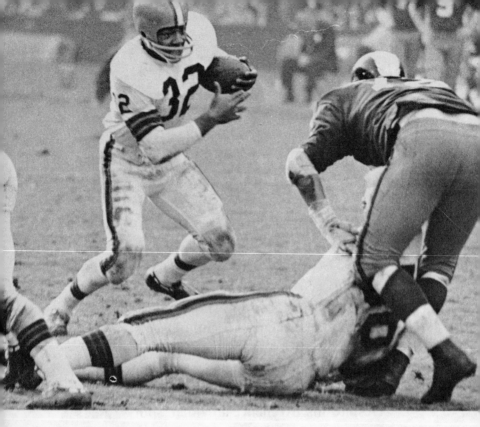

Brown sizes up a Redskin defender on his way around end.

long touchdown run. When he came back to the bench, Paul Brown, the Cleveland coach, told him, "You're my fullback." Ed Modzelewski, who had been Cleveland's regular fullback, said later that he felt like a substitute for Babe Ruth.

The Browns won the Eastern Conference

championship in Jim's rookie year. His biggest day of the season — and one of the greatest of his career — came on November 24, 1957, when the Browns, leading the Eastern Conference by one game, met a strong Los Angeles Rams team.

Tommy O'Connell, the Cleveland quarterback, was hurt early in the first quarter, placing an extra burden on Brown. Jim scored twice in the first period. His second score came on a 68-yard run. But in the third quarter Jim fumbled, giving the Rams a chance to score. They did and took a commanding 28-17 lead.

Embarrassed by the fumble, Brown came back strong. In less than four minutes, he slammed into the end zone from close range after a 34-yard run, then fought his way into the end zone again for another score. A 45-yard run in the fourth period set up another Cleveland touchdown. The Browns won, 45-31, and Jim Brown established a new single-game rushing record. He had carried the ball 31 times for 237 yards. In addition he had scored four touchdowns and set up two touchdowns and a field goal.

Cleveland lost the 1957 championship game to Detroit. In 1958 they tied the New York Giants for the Eastern Conference title, and Brown set a new league rushing record with a total of 1,527 yards. He also led the league in scoring with 108 points on 18 touchdowns. But his accomplishments were offset by Cleveland's loss to the Giants in the playoff game where Jim was held to eight yards in seven carries.

In each of the next five years the Browns finished second or third in the Eastern Conference. But Brown continued to lead the league in rushing yardage. During some seasons it seemed that Jim was 90 per cent of Cleveland's offense. Soon opposing defensive men keyed on Brown. They knew that if they could stop him they could stop the whole Cleveland attack. The Browns had no effective passing attack to balance their one-man running attack.

In 1962 it appeared that the years of carrying the heavy load were beginning to catch up with the mighty Brown. His rushing yardage sagged below 1,000—to 996 — for the first time since his rookie season. Magazines published stories asking if Jim Brown was washed up. Rushing yardage of 996 would be phenomenal for an ordinary player but not for Brown.

Jim breaks loose for a long gain as linebacker Sam Huff makes a lunging try to tackle him.

To make matters worse, Paul Brown, the coach, and Jim Brown, the star, were not seeing eye to eye. The coach needled Jim in public statements, and Jim resented it. He had injured his left wrist early in the season and had been forced to use his right arm, instead of his left, to ward off tacklers. But he kept quiet about the injury because he didn't want to make excuses.

In the 1963 Pro Bowl Game at Los Angeles, after the close of the 1962 season, Jim was healthy again. Stung by the claims that he was "washed up," he ripped the West's defense for 144 yards on 17 carries. For the second straight year he was voted the Pro Bowl's Most Valuable Player.

"I knew I wasn't through," he told reporters. "You can't play one hundred per cent when you're hurt. Maybe I convinced some people that I still have it."

Paul Brown was replaced as Cleveland coach by Blanton Collier before the 1963 season. Jim responded to the change by setting a new rushing record of 1,863 yards. Collier had installed a new offense that gave Brown a chance to do more running to the outside, and Brown was happy again.

There still was one goal that Brown had never reached. He had never played on a league championship team. For years critics had discounted his yardage records by saying, "The Browns never will win a championship with Jim. He isn't a team player." Jim resented being called a show-off. He had told sportswriters that he would gladly trade in his own records for just one championship. But the critics continued to berate him.

With Collier at the helm and a new spirit in the ball club, a championship finally seemed to be within reach in 1964. The Browns had acquired Ernie Green to share some of the heavy ballcarrying and Paul Warfield to help with the pass-receiving chores. In addition, they had Frank Ryan, a fine passer, calling the plays at quarterback.

The Browns finally did go all the way. Jim's achievements of other years seemed insignificant compared with his help in winning a league title for Cleveland. The championship game against the Baltimore Colts at Cleveland Stadium was one of the most important games in Brown's career.

The Colts were favored, but Cleveland won easily, 27-0. It was a team victory, pure and simple.

Pass receiver Gary Collins and Frank Ryan were the heroes. But Jim Brown had played his part and had proven that he was a team player.

Cleveland won the Eastern Conference title again in 1965, with room to spare. They met an inspired Green Bay team in the championship game on a cold snowy afternoon in Green Bay. Brown had trouble with his footing in the snow and mud. Meanwhile, Packer backs Paul Hornung and Jim Taylor had a good day and received the recognition that is usually reserved for Brown. The Packers won.

The loss of the championship game did not obscure Jim's usual great contribution to the Browns. Without him, they might never have reached the championship game. One of his best performances was against the New York Giants. On that day in Yankee Stadium his playing was superb. He smashed into the Giant line and secondary 24 times for 177 yards. He caught three passes for 18 more yards. To crown the day, he threw a 23-yard touchdown pass to Collins.

Every time Brown gains a yard, he breaks his own all-time NFL records. Every touchdown he scores is a new high. Brown passed the all-time

A good runner always follows his blockers. Here Monte Clark clears the way for Brown.

rushing record (set by Joe Perry) in the middle of the 1963 season. At the end of the 1965 season, he had gained 12,312 yards by rushing — 4,000 more than his nearest competitor. His total yardage (including pass receptions and kick-off and punt returns) through 1965 was 15,459 yards — nearly, nine miles in nine years. During his first nine years in the NFL, he has won the rushing title eight times. Only his loss of the title to Jim Taylor of Green Bay in 1962 kept him from having a perfect record. None of the other great runners in professional football has ever come close to winning the rushing award eight times.

Brown's records fill the yearbooks of the NFL. But statistics are dull and lifeless. A real appreciation of his talents comes from watching him follow his blockers through a narrow hole, slide away from a would-be tackler and then open the throttle when he gets a glimpse of daylight. Statistics cannot tell how Brown takes a pitchout from Frank Ryan or a short screen pass and then turns on the speed as he cuts across the field with his jarring power.

How hard does Jim Brown hit? Ask the giants on the NFL's defensive units. They know from

Brown charges through a small hole in the Eagles' line.

experience that it hurts when he runs into a tackler and then breaks away. At six-foot-two and weighing 228 pounds, he is not as big as some other NFL fullbacks. But when a tackler gets near him, Brown's bulging shoulders twist, the 32-inch waist seems to slip away and his amazing thigh and calf muscles seem always to have the power for one more drive.

After a play Brown walks back to the huddle with a deceptively lazy manner. His face reflects neither pain nor joy on the football field. Jim believes in the stoic, spartan approach to the game.

"Why do you always get up so slowly?" Brown was asked at a football luncheon.

"I like to have a man think he might have hurt me," Brown replied. "That makes it hard for the other fellow to know when I really am hurt. It keeps them guessing."

When Cleveland picked Jim Brown as their first choice in the 1956 college draft, Coach Paul Brown said, "We hope he will be the next Marion Motley."

The next Marion Motley, indeed. Motley had been a great fullback for the Browns in the early 1950s. But Jim Brown was not going to become the

Jim pauses for a drink of water.

next anybody. When he finally retires he will leave records that should last for decades. Nobody talks about Brown's being "another Marion Motley" any more. Many think that not even Bronko Nagurski, Ernie Nevers or Jim Thorpe can compare to him. He has outdistanced all his competitors and now plays in a class all by himself. NFL coaches hope that someday they will find a fullback they can call "another Jimmy Brown."

STEVE VAN BUREN
chapter two

When Steve Van Buren was a high-school boy in New Orleans he wanted to be a prize fighter. His uncle, a fight fan, encouraged him and made plans to become his manager. But then a football bid from Louisiana State University persuaded Steve to forget the ring. "My uncle was so mad at me he didn't speak to me for almost a year," he said years later.

Born in Tela, Honduras, in 1921, Van Buren became an orphan at an early age and was sent to New Orleans to live with his grandparents.

He saw his first football game while he was a

student at Warren Easton High School in New Orleans. He wanted to try out for the team, but he weighed only 125 pounds. The coach wouldn't let him try out; he was afraid Steve would get hurt.

Steve quit school after his sophomore year and went to work in an iron foundry. But he soon returned to school, having grown to a muscular 155 pounds in the meantime. He was well on the way to becoming the six-foot-one, 208-pounder he would be during his professional football days. His play in the final two years of high school caught the attention of the coaches at Louisiana State, and he was offered a scholarship. He gave up his boxing ambitions to attend LSU, where he majored in mechanical engineering.

The LSU coaches used Van Buren as a blocking back during his freshman and sophomore years. Alvin Dark, who would one day become a major league baseball player and manager, was the LSU tailback and did most of the running and throwing for the Bayou Tigers.

At LSU, Steve thought he was a better baseball player than Dark. But the LSU coaching staff took him off the baseball team so that he could work out on the track team. "They had me

Eagle coach Greasy Neale presents the game ball to Van Buren after a winning effort.

run the hundred yards," Steve recalls. "I was the world's fastest human for about sixty yards, and then they started to go past me. If there were ten in the race, nine would catch me by the ninety-eighth yard."

When Al Dark went into service, Van Buren took over the running-back position. He had a good senior year, gaining 832 yards. At the end of the season he was the first choice of the Philadelphia Eagles in the annual draft of college players. Somebody in the Eagles' scouting department had seen Van Buren at LSU. The scout had turned in a glowing report on the square-jawed, chunky halfback and convinced the Eagles to make him their first choice. It was the best draft they ever made.

"I had never heard of the Eagles," Van Buren has said. "We didn't pay so much attention to pro ball down there in those days. In fact, when they sent me my railroad ticket to Philadelphia, I rode right past the North Philadelphia station and wound up in New York."

In 1944 the United States was deeply involved in World War II, and most of the NFL players were serving in the armed forces. Van Buren had been rejected by the services because of a chronic eye ailment. He got an immediate chance to prove his worth as a football player since there were few talented players available to play.

In his rookie year Van Buren carried the ball 80 times for 444 yards and averaged 5.5 yards per carry, a good enough record to earn him fifth ranking among the league's rushers. An appendectomy forced him out of action for several games, making his achievement all the more impressive. The Eagles finished second in the Eastern Conference.

With his rookie year behind him, Van Buren really came into his own in 1945 and led the NFL ground-gainers with a total of 832 yards. He set an Eagles' club record that still stands by scoring 18 touchdowns — 16 on runs and 2 on passes. Despite Steve's sensational performance, the Eagles finished second again. In 1946 Steve was slowed down by injuries. He lost the rushing crown to Bill Dudley of Pittsburgh, and the Eagles finished second for the third straight year.

Steve was one of those "give me the ball" players, an eye-catching combination of raw power, speed and guile. He was blessed with a tremendous chest and wide, powerful shoulders,

Van Buren carries around end in a 1?

and his body tapered down to the slim legs of a track man. He had the elusiveness of a Red Grange and the crashing power of a Bronko Nagurski.

One day Van Buren collided with a teammate,

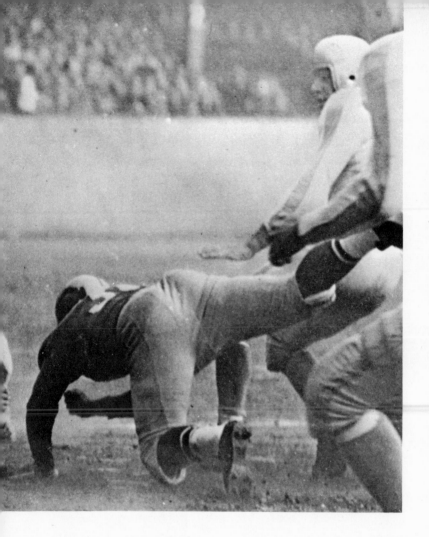

ie against the New York Bulldogs.

Jack Ferrante, on a missed assignment. Ferrante
was knocked dizzy. As he picked himself off the
ground, an opponent walked over to him and said,
"It hurts doesn't it? Now you know how it feels

when you try to tackle that guy."

One of Steve's favorite plays was the slant over right tackle — a power play. But he also had a magnificent head and shoulder fake and was able to start wide, as though on an end sweep, pivot on his big toe and slant back inside. Van Buren was famous for his "second effort," his ability to gain more yardage after he had apparently been stopped by a tackler.

In the last game of the 1947 season, Steve was trying to break the NFL rushing record set by Beattie Feathers, the great back of the Chicago Bears. After he finally crashed once more through the line and broke Feathers' record by four yards, he surprised everyone by running off the field and telling the coach, "We've got it won. Let the subs play." It was the first time that anyone could remember Van Buren's wanting to come out of a game.

Steve's record-breaking performance helped the Eagles win their first Eastern Conference title in 1947. Philadelphia finished the regular season in a tie with Pittsburgh and then beat the Steelers 21-0 in a playoff game.

In the championship game, the Eagles played

the tough Chicago Cardinals on a frozen field at Comiskey Park in Chicago. Steve was held to 26 yards in 18 carries, although he scored one touchdown on a one-yard plunge in the third quarter. The Eagles lost 28-21.

In 1948 the Eagles rushed through the Eastern Conference with a 9-2-1 record and got their chance for revenge on the Cardinals in the NFL title game at Shibe Park in Philadelphia.

A raging blizzard swept through Philadelphia on the day of the game. Since there was no modern snow removal equipment, the snow had to be removed by hand. Workmen toiled for hours, tugging at the snow-covered tarpaulin and piling up huge snowbanks along the fringe of the playing field. Since the borders of the field were invisible, the sidelines were roped off. The officials used the chains to measure first downs in the absence of the snow-covered yard lines.

The Cardinals had beaten the Eagles 28-21 during the regular season and were favored to repeat their victory in the championship game. The teams struggled through nearly three quarters with no score. With seconds remaining in the third period, the Eagles got a break. Bucko Kilroy

recovered a Cardinal fumble on the Cards' 17. In one play before the end of the quarter, the Eagles gained six yards. Then both teams moved to the other side of the field.

New snow had obliterated all markers at the new end of the field. Joe Muha made three yards over center on the next play. Then quarterback Tommy Thompson ran the quarterback sneak. He moved the ball to the five-yard line and gained the first down. On the next play Thompson handed off

In the 1948 championship game Van Buren slogs around and for a long gain.

to Van Buren. Steve slogged through the snow and over the goal line for the only score of a 7-0 game. Despite the near-impossible conditions, Steve had carried the ball 26 times for 98 yards.

"Run, that's all he wanted to do," said Greasy Neale, who coached the Eagles from 1944 through 1950. "He was a fair kicker, and he could have been a better one. He was not bad at catching passes, but all he wanted to practice was running. Steve was every bit as fast and elusive as Red

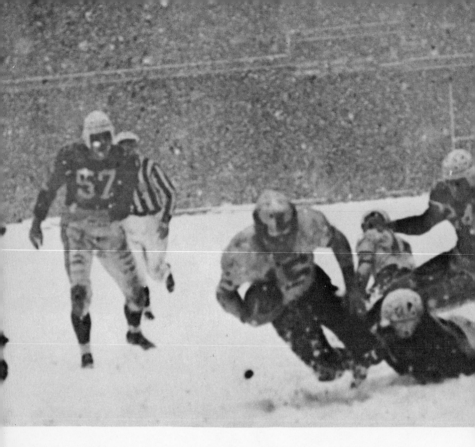

Grange. Only he didn't need blockers like Red did. He could run over people just like Bronko Nagurski."

Van Buren did score several touchdowns by catching passes from Tommy Thompson, but he always considered the forward pass as something to be tried when the run didn't work. "The fellow who threw the first pass must have been all through or just too tired to run with the ball," he once said.

Van Buren scores the only touchdown of the championship game to give the Eagles the title.

The reign of the Eagles lasted one more year. In 1949 they rushed through the Eastern Conference, winning eleven games and losing one. Their only loss was to the Chicago Bears in an interconference game.

Steve was at the peak of his career. He smashed through defenses for a record-breaking total of 1,146 yards on 263 carries, setting an NFL record that stood until Jim Brown gained 1,527 yards in 1958.

In a game against the New York Bulldogs, Van Buren carried the ball 35 times. The next week against Pittsburgh he carried 27 times and gained 205 yards, becoming one of the few men in the NFL to gain more than 200 yards in a single game.

This time the championship game was to be played in the home city of the Western Conference winners, the Los Angeles Rams. The Eagles heaved a sigh of relief. No snow this year, they thought. But it poured rain in Los Angeles, and the field was heavy with mud when the teams took the field before only 27,980 fans in the vast Coliseum.

Once again Van Buren proved himself under the worst possible conditions. By blasting through the Rams' defense for 196 yards on 31 carries, he set a record that still stands for an NFL championship game. Ram quarterback Bob Waterfield's passing attack was blunted by the rain, and the Eagles won, 14-0.

The pro teams played a basic five-man line on defense instead of the four-man lines common today. But they often shifted to seven-man lines to stop Van Buren.

"I'd just love to run against those four-man lines they have nowadays," Van Buren said recently. "I certainly wouldn't gain less than I did. It was tough just getting past the line in those days. Now, if one lineman is blocked out, you have space to run before that linebacker can move up to take you.

"Running is easier nowadays because of the diversification of the offense and the development of the forward pass," Van Buren continued. "When I played I never got to run such a thing as a draw play (the play in which the quarterback runs back, fakes a pass and hands off to the charging fullback). It was mostly off-tackle plays and end runs. You went both ways in those days, too. I played defense when we didn't have the ball. You had to try to pace yourself a little."

After the 1949 championship, Van Buren's career was all downhill. He was injured in the preseason College All-Star Game in 1950 and limped through the regular season. He gained only 629 yards and lost his rushing title to Marion Motley of the Cleveland Browns. The Browns had just been admitted to the NFL in 1950. They forecast the end of the Eagles' success by defeating them 35-10 in the very first game of the season.

Van Buren's playing career came to a sudden

end during the 1952 training season. A rookie end missed his assignment on a play and collided with Van Buren, causing him to rupture a ligament in his left knee. The great back could no longer pivot on his left foot. He wisely retired from the sport and never played another game.

After his active career ended, Van Buren worked for the Eagles as a talent scout and public relations adviser. In recent years he has coached the Newark Bears in the minor leagues.

If Steve were playing football in the 1960s, he would give Jim Brown a run for his money. He set most of the NFL ground-gaining records that Brown broke and is the only man except Brown to win the rushing title three years in a row. Most impressive, he set his records when NFL defenses were aimed at runners, not passers. Modern teams can always threaten a pass to keep defenses "loose" and then give the ball to a runner. Van Buren ran straight into a defense that was ready for him. Still he managed to give his team two championships and to rewrite the NFL record books.

RED
GRANGE
chapter
three

Have you ever wondered what professional football was like in the days before television brought the Sunday games into everyone's home and before every newspaper was filled with stories about the Packers, the Bears, the Giants and the Browns?

In the early 1920s, professional football didn't attract big crowds of 70,000 and 80,000. Nobody dreamed of paying players thousands of dollars just to play football on Sunday afternoons. Television had not been invented, and even radio was new and untested. The players were paid $10 or $25 a game. They worked at other jobs all week and played football on Saturday and Sunday. Often they played with two different teams under different names in the same weekend. The same man would be Charley Smith in Frankford, Pennsylvania, on Saturday and Harry Kelly in Rochester, New York, on Sunday.

If an opposing team offered to pay more money, a player could switch teams in the middle of the season. A star as famous as Jim Brown is today might play with Cleveland one week and with the New York Giants the next week. Some players didn't wear helmets. They played bareheaded, with only a thick matting of hair to pad their heads. Face guards and safety equipment had not even been invented.

Instead of charging admission, the owner of a professional team often took up a collection, passing through the crowd at half time with a hat. Sometimes he didn't take in enough money to pay the players. After he had paid for the uniforms, the rental of the park and the train fare, he and the players would divide what was left.

The first all-professional team played at Latrobe, Pennsylvania, in the fall of 1895. Each

Red Grange follows a play from the sidelines.

player received $10 to play for the Latrobe Y.M.C.A. in a game against a nearby town. Soon other teams of professional players were organized in the coal and steel towns of western Pennsylvania and eastern Ohio.

When the National Football League was organized in 1921, each team put up a $100 entrance fee. Although the organization of a league with stronger rules about player contracts did stablilize the game, professional football remained a haphazard sport. Players were still poorly paid, and the fans continued to be more interested in baseball and college football.

The man who changed all this was Red Grange, the Galloping Ghost from Illinois. He was Jimmy Brown and Johnny Unitas all rolled into one — a superstar who almost singlehandedly changed professional football from a disorganized local game to a glamorous national sport.

Grange played most of his football during the Golden Age of Sport — the 1920s. In 1927, Babe Ruth hit 60 home runs for the Yankees. Jack Dempsey, the heavyweight boxing champion, was a national celebrity. Bobby Jones was winning all the major golf tournaments and was making golf a popular game for rich and poor alike. But Grange had a special problem. Although many sports fans followed college football, few of them had ever been to a professional game. It remained for Grange to prove that football was not just a game for college boys.

Red was born in Pennsylvania on June 13, 1903. When he was a young boy, his father moved the family to Wheaton, Illinois. In high school, Red was a 16-letter man, winning letters all four years in basketball, baseball, football and track. At some track meets, Red won the 100-yard dash, the 220, the low hurdles, the high jump and the broad jump all in the same day. In baseball he was good enough to receive a contract offer from the old Boston Braves. But he really excelled in football. In his four years with the Wheaton High School team Red scored 75 touchdowns and kicked 82 extra points for a total of 532 points.

"My father was the one who insisted I go to college," said Grange many years later. "If it hadn't been for him I probably never would have continued after high school."

But athletes couldn't expect full scholarships in those days, so Red had to work to make enough money for college. The owner of an ice company in Wheaton offered Red a summer job at $37.50 a week. Since no one had electric refrigerators then, an ice man came around every other day in a truck or wagon. Red's job was to carry 50 and 100-pound blocks of ice up to each house and to place them in the customers' ice boxes. Years later, sportswriters would call him "The Wheaton Iceman."

A graduate of the University of Michigan tried to talk Red into going to Michigan. But he finally decided on Illinois on the recommendation of George Dawson, a neighbor who played football there.

When the Illinois varsity played the freshman team in the fall of 1922, Red ran through them as easily as he had run through the high-school teams that had played Wheaton. Bob Zuppke, the Illinois coach, was quick to notice, and he prepared Red for a varsity assignment the next year.

Grange played his first varsity game against Nebraska in September, 1923. He displayed the know-how of a veteran. Picking out every hole in the defense and swinging past Nebraska tacklers like a hula dancer when he broke into the open field, he scored three touchdowns on runs of 35, 65 and 14 yards and became a national sensation overnight.

By the end of his sophomore year, Grange had scored 12 touchdowns and gained 1,260 yards. Walter Camp, who picked the official All-America team in those days, chose Red as the left halfback on the first team, a sensational success for a sophomore.

Illinois and Michigan did not play each other during 1923, and both teams finished the season with perfect records in the Big Ten, tying for the championship. Their scheduled game early in the 1924 season was to be the test of the two great teams, and it attracted more attention than most bowl games do today. Sports writers came from as far away as New York and California to see if what they heard about the Wheaton Iceman was true.

Illinois coach Bob Zuppke had carefully set the stage for a spectacular performance by Grange. In the opening game against Nebraska he had let Red play the entire game without scoring. Time after time he instructed Grange to run to the sidelines without cutting back. Nebraska boxed him in against the sideline while scouts from

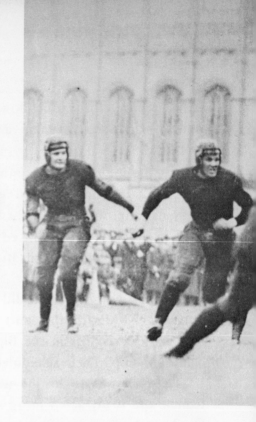

Grange carries the ball in the 1924 Illinois-Chicago game. Red scored three touchdowns, but called it the toughest game he ever played. Final score: 21-21.

Michigan took notes on how Grange had been stopped. Grange followed the same strategy in the second game against Butler.

Meanwhile, Zuppke taught Grange a new running pattern that looked on paper like an inverted "S." Grange was to swing toward one sideline, cut back to the opposite side and then reverse his field again while moving toward the goal. The redhead worked hard on the new pattern.

A few days before the game, Fielding Yost, the great Michigan coach, told newsmen, "Mr. Grange will be a carefully watched young man. Every time he takes the ball there will be just about eleven clean, hard Michigan tacklers headed his way." Zuppke whipped up the Illinois team, Grange in particular, by mailing clippings of Yost's remarks to all members of the squad.

When Michigan lined up against Illinois in the big game on October 18, the Michigan captain,

Red (at left) heads for a touchdown against Mich.

is won 39-14 and Grange accounted for all Illinois touchdowns.

preparing to kick off, asked tauntingly, "Which one is Grange?" Of course everybody in Memorial Stadium knew that Grange was Number 77. The number had already become nationally famous.

The Michigan captain kicked to Grange, and Red started for the near sideline where the Michigan defense was waiting for him. Instead of continuing into their hands, he cut back to the opposite side and then back again on a 95-yard touchdown run.

That was just the beginning.

Before the end of the first quarter, Grange galloped 67 yards for a second touchdown, 56 yards for a third and 44 yards for a fourth. He scored four touchdowns in the first 12 minutes of the first quarter, the most spectacular performance by any player before or since.

Red came back after a rest and scored a fifth touchdown in the second half and also threw a touchdown pass. Illinois defeated Michigan 39-14, with Red Grange accounting for all six of their touchdowns. In his account of the game, Grantland Rice, the nation's top sportswriter, called Grange "The Galloping Ghost," a nickname that stayed with him for the rest of his career.

Grange scored 13 touchdowns in his junior year and six more as a senior. In his three years at Illinois he scored 31 touchdowns and gained 4,280 yards — nearly 2 1/2 miles. Although his senior year was not as good as the first two, Red left Eastern fans goggle-eyed when he ripped through a strong University of Pennsylvania team for three scores and 363 yards in 36 carries on a muddy field in Philadelphia. This was his only appearance in the East, where football fans still believed that their teams were superior to those who played "out on the prairies."

Long before Red played his last college game, he had begun to think of professional football. He had acquired a manager, Charles C. Pyle, a man who owned a series of movie theaters in central Illinois. Prolonged negotiations between Pyle, later known as Cold Cash Pyle from his initials and his hard bargaining, and George Halas, the owner of the Chicago Bears, resulted in an agreement for Grange to join the Chicago Bears after the close of the Illinois season.

After the last Illinois game, Red sneaked down a fire escape, grabbed a train to Chicago and registered under an assumed name in a Chicago hotel. Later that same night Pyle and Halas reached agreement. Grange was to get half the money the Bears would make in their remaining regular and exhibition games. In turn, he was to split his half with Pyle.

Grange sat on the Bears' bench the day after his last game at Illinois. On the following Thursday, which was Thanksgiving Day, he appeared with the Bears in their all-Chicago rivalry with the old Chicago (now St. Louis) Cardinals.

The punter for the Cardinals managed to kick the ball away from Grange all afternoon so that he would have no chance for a spectacular run-back. Although Red's debut was not sensational, a sellout crowd of 36,000 gave him a great ovation and mobbed him for autographs after the game.

In those days many people did not consider pro football a proper profession for a collegian. There had been many newspaper editorials against Grange's plans to turn pro. He explained his decision in these words: "I am going into professional football to make money. I see nothing wrong with it. It seems to be the same as playing professional baseball. I am still loyal to Illinois, but I don't think I owe the college any more."

Pro football was not the closely knit organization it is today. The NFL was made up of 20 teams. Some league teams played as many as 20 games while others played only six or seven. Schedules were always subject to change.

With Grange as a super drawing attraction, Halas, then the playing coach of the Bears, drew up a back-breaking schedule of regular-season and exhibition games. In a period of 18 days, the Bears scheduled 10 games. After the Thanksgiving Day game with the Cardinals, the Bears rested two days, then played Columbus on Sunday. They played in St. Louis on Wednesday, Frankford, Pennsylvania, on Saturday and then headed for New York to play the Giants.

Tim Mara, owner of the Giants, was just about ready to disband his team. He had lost about $200,000 and could not afford to lose much more. He was understandably eager to see if Red Grange could attract a larger crowd.

The day of Grange's first appearance in New York dawned cold and clear. Before noon the 3,000 extra police assigned to handle the crowds lost control of the throng pushing into the Polo Grounds. Outside the park, tickets were sold for three to four times their face value. Fans stormed the gates and climbed up ladders which they had set against the bleacher wall. They jammed the upper and lower stands, spilled into the stairways and poured into the emergency stands on the field.

The crowd was estimated at 70,000 people. Grange didn't let them down. When he scored a touchdown on a pass interception, the crowd went wild. Red picked up a check for $40,000 as his part of the tremendous gate. Mr. Mara paid many of his debts with his proceeds, and the Giants were on the way to becoming one of the most successful franchises in the NFL.

Within a few weeks after turning professional, Red Grange had electrified the country. He had attracted crowds in numbers that no one dreamed possible and had saved a nearly bankrupt team in New York. Professional football had come of age.

The wild Grange tour continued with games Tuesday in Washington, Wednesday in Boston, Thursday in Pittsburgh, Saturday in Detroit and Sunday back in Chicago. Red suffered a serious injury to his left arm in the Pittsburgh game and had to sit out the Detroit contest. As a result the management had to refund about $20,000.

Grange poses during his professional career. His name has been scrawled on his left pant leg.

During this frantic tour, the players wore the same mud-caked uniforms day after day and took their shower baths in one tiny bathroom on a Pullman car. They arrived back in Chicago utterly exhausted, but everyone had made money and Grange had pocketed $105,000.

Encouraged by the success of this trip, Halas and Pyle booked the Bears on another long tour that took them to Coral Gables, Florida (where tickets sold for $19.80 apiece), Tampa, New Orleans, Los Angeles, San Francisco, Seattle and Portland. They played 19 games in about five weeks, and Grange had over $200,000 to show for his efforts.

Grange wanted a one-third interest in the Bears as his fee for playing with them in 1926, but owner George Halas refused. So Pyle and Grange started their own league. Grange played for the New York team which was known as the Yankees and played its home games at Yankee Stadium. But the league failed after one year and the Yankees, owned by C. C. Pyle, became part of the NFL.

Playing for the Yankees against the Bears in 1927, Grange suffered a twisted right knee in a pile-up. He never was the same again. Although he returned to the Bears in 1929, after sitting out the 1928 season because of the injury, Grange never regained his old form. His amazing speed and elusiveness were gone, but even so he remained with the Bears through 1934. In 1931 he even made the first NFL All-Star Team as a left halfback, and in the 1932 title game with Portsmouth, Ohio, Grange caught a short jump pass from Bronko Nagurski for the winning touchdown. In the 1933 championship game against New York, the redhead made a game-saving tackle.

Although Grange was not the same Galloping Ghost in his later years with the Bears, he developed into a fine pass receiver and blocker. He was often used as the man in motion to decoy the defenses away from the middle of the line. This opened the way for bull-like rushes through the middle by the Bears' fullback, Bronko Nagurski.

Grange played his last game on January 27, 1935, in an exhibition against the Giants in Los Angeles. The Bears had set it up for Red to finish off his career with a touchdown run, but he was caught from behind by a 250-pound Giant lineman. Grange knew that he was finished.

Grange went into the insurance business and remained active in football as a radio and television braodcaster with the Bears until 1964. Then he retired to Florida, where he operates a real-estate business.

The Wheaton Iceman has been elected to both the college and professional football Halls of Fame, and his accomplishments on the field have become legendary. But perhaps his greatest accomplishment was changing professional football almost overnight from a sand-lot game to a new national pastime.

JIM
TAYLOR
chapter
four

On January 2, 1966, a bone-chilling wind whipped from Lake Michigan through Green Bay. Swirling snow shut down the airport and covered early morning churchgoers with a blanket of white.

At Curly Lambeau Stadium, where the Packers were to play the Cleveland Browns for the championship of the National Football League, a small army of men had started work at dawn. A thick field cover of straw had been removed by a score of men with pitchforks. Another crew was busy rolling up the tarpaulin. But then the snow started again.

Jim Taylor grinned when he stepped out of his car and moved into the Packers' dressing room. "It's Packer weather," he said to Jerry Kramer and Fuzzy Thurston, other running guards, whose lockers were next to his.

Outside, a helicopter hovered just a few feet above the field, trying to blow four inches of fresh snow off the playing surface. Two bulldozers from the city's sanitation department crisscrossed the field, pushing the snow into huge banks along the sidelines.

By the time Taylor and his Packer mates were ready to come out for their warm-up, the bulldozers had done their job. But it was still snowing. Soon the yard lines were obliterated, and it was impossible to see the yard markers on the sidelines. The officials agreed they would use yard chains to determine first downs.

Willie Wood and Herb Adderley, two Packer defensive backs, engaged in a brief snowball fight while Taylor and Paul Hornung, his running mate, tried the footing. Quarterback Bart Starr, who had a sore shoulder, wore a deep scowl as he tried to throw the wet, slippery football.

Jim Brown and the Cleveland Browns looked

Jim Taylor takes a rest during the championship game in January, 1966.

disgusted. He ran gingerly for a few steps and slid in the snow. His face was solemn. He had been afraid of bad weather in Green Bay for weeks.

Governor Warren Knowles of Wisconsin had flown up from the capital at Madison to see the game, but his plane couldn't land in the heavy snowstorm. Word came over the radio that he had returned to Madison and would settle for watching the game on television.

But 50,852 others appeared at Lambeau Stadium. They clawed at the wet snow to uncover their seats. Long lines of traffic backed up for miles around the stadium. One lady slipped and broke a leg but refused to go to the hospital until the game was over. Packer fans were used to rough weather and hardship.

Cleveland's attack leaned heavily on the running of Jim Brown, whose rushing total for the regular season had been 1,544 yards, almost 800 yards better than his closest challenger. Brown's running and the passes of Frank Ryan to Gary Collins and Paul Warfield represented Cleveland's threat. Green Bay counted on Starr's passes and the powerful running of Taylor and Hornung.

It was a close game for the first half. But a Packer touchdown on a 13-yard run by Paul

Packer stars Taylor and Hornung carry coach Vince Lombardi off the field after their victory over Cleveland in the championship game.

Hornung and a blocked Browns' field goal decided the outcome early in the third quarter. The final score was Green Bay 23, Cleveland 12.

Taylor had carried the ball 27 times and had churned over the slippery turf for 96 yards. Hornung had carried 18 times for 105 yards. Jim Brown had been held to 50 yards on 12 attempts. Taylor and Hornung carried grinning Packer coach Vince Lombardi off the field on their shoulders.

"I guess we'll let Jimmy keep Number 31 now," said Fuzzy Thurston in the steaming dressing room. "For a while we were thinking of giving it to Grabowski."

He smiled at his joke. The Packers had just signed two high-priced rookies from the college draft. One of them, Jim Grabowski of Illinois, who had worn Taylor's "31" in college, was supposed to be in line to take Jim's fullback job. There had been talk during 1965 that Taylor was on the way out. But his performance against the Browns had shown again that he planned to stay on the Packers' regular team.

A muddy troupe from the press box brought the word that Taylor had been voted the Most Valuable Player in the game and was the winner of a brand new sports car.

"Didn't I tell you, Jimmy?" shouted Jerry Kramer. "I told you you'd have a great afternoon. You ought to share that car with me."

Lombardi, melted snow glistening on the protective cover over his hat, was all over the room, shaking hands with his team, slapping this fellow across the back, poking another in the ribs. "A lot of people counted them out," Lombardi said, pointing to Taylor and Hornung. "I guess that proves there is a little life in the old boys yet."

When they asked Lombardi if he thought the challenge of playing against Jim Brown had contributed to Taylor's fine day, he said, "Jim has a lot of pride. This was the ordinary reaction for a man who's got pride. He always rises to the occasion."

At first Taylor denied the competition with Brown. But when he was pressed, he winked and cocked his head. "I was conscious of what he (Brown) was doing. I knew we were playing Cleveland. Nobody had to tell me who he was."

Taylor has been running second best to Jim Brown throughout his career, except for one year (1962) when he led the NFL rushing with 1,474 yards. Brown is the only man in the history of the league to make more yards in a year, but he has done it three times, in 1958, 1963 and 1965.

In direct competition with Brown, Taylor has more than held his own. The Packers and Browns seldom meet during the regular season because Green Bay is in the Western Conference and Cleveland is in the Eastern Conference. But since Brown and Taylor came into the league, the two

teams have met four times.

In 1961 Taylor had a field day against Cleveland, scoring four touchdowns and rolling up 158 yards on 21 attempts. Brown gained only 72 yards on 16 carries. The two met again at

Taylor gallops through a gaping hole on his way to a fourth touchdown against the Browns in 1961.

Milwaukee in a regular-season game in 1964. Taylor scored two touchdowns, and the Packers won again 28-21. When Cleveland played Green Bay in the play-off Bowl Game in January, 1964, the Packers' Bart Starr riddled Cleveland with his passes, and neither Taylor nor Brown was outstanding in a game won by Green Bay 40-23. Then in the 1965 championship game, Taylor won the Most Valuable Player award, and Green Bay won the championship.

If it were not for Brown, Taylor would be hailed as the outstanding running back of football. His rushing total of 7,502 yards gives him third place in the all-time standings. Joe Perry, now retired, gained 8,378, a total which Taylor may surpass. But Brown's 12,312 yards leaves him all alone in first place.

Taylor is the perfect fullback type. When he churns those heavily muscled legs, hunches his muscular shoulders and drives into the opponent's line, he is almost impossible to stop. Some observers insist that he cannot be brought down if he is hit between the knee and hips. He has the well-trained body of a fighter. "No one hits me harder than I hit them," he has said. He is known for his dogged determination to keep going. He refuses to stop even when he is hit.

"I used to be stiff and bullish," Taylor said. "I tried to run over everybody. Now I try to go where the blockers tell me."

Jim drags a Forty-Niner tackler toward the goal.

There still are times when Taylor tries to run over a tackler on a one-on-one situation. Off the field, he is a quiet man with an easy smile, but he is a dedicated wildcat when he is in action. He still likes to "sting" people, meaning that he prefers to jolt a would-be tackler instead of running around him.

"He gives you the impression that you are not supposed to tackle him," said one veteran NFL linebacker. "You have to hit him and keep on hitting. If you let up, he'll keep right on going. The officials give him a slow whistle, and you have to knock him down sometimes after the whistle to be sure he is going to stay down."

When the Packers played the New York Giants in the 1962 championship game at windy Yankee Stadium, there was a major controversy about the way Sam Huff, then with the Giants, handled Taylor. Sam especially liked to play rough against Taylor, who often taunts an opponent with a jeering, "Is that as hard as you can hit?" The other defensive players in the league agreed that Huff's play had been rough but clean. Taylor and some other offensive fullbacks complained that Huff had gone too far in piling on after a play had been stopped.

Like Steve Van Buren fifteen years earlier, Taylor came from Louisiana State University. He was born in Baton Rouge, Louisiana, the home of LSU, on September 20, 1935. His father died when he was only 10. While attending grammar school and high school, he helped support his family by peddling papers at four o'clock each morning.

At Baton Rouge High School Jim was a top basketball player and also a football star. After graduating from high school, he entered LSU.

As a junior at LSU in 1956, he led the Southeastern Conference in scoring with 59 points. As a senior, he scored 86 points in 10 games, placing third in the nation. In addition to running the ball, he also kicked conversions.

Taylor was the Packers' second draft choice in 1958, but he failed to impress Scooter McLean, the head coach. He was almost cut from the squad but was saved when another rookie back, Dick Christy, had a bad day in the final exhibition and was cut instead. McLean used Taylor only on the kickoff and punt-return teams until late in the season. When Jim finally got a chance to run with

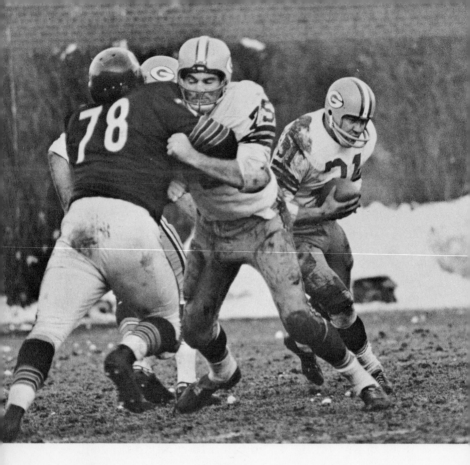

the ball he bulled his way for 247 yards in games against the San Francisco Forty-Niners and the Los Angeles Rams.

Vince Lombardi took over the Packer coaching job in 1959. "Jim was not much of a blocker," recalled Lombardi. "But he had fine balance and you could tell that he loved to hit."

Taylor fitted into Lombardi's plans for rebuilding the Packers with young, dedicated

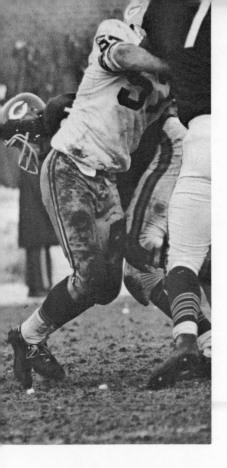

The Packer line opens up another hole for Taylor.

players. He played a major part in early season victories over Chicago and Detroit but then sustained a freak injury at home that put him out for half the season.

Jim's wife, Dixie, was preparing dinner at their apartment when the grease she was heating to make french fried potatoes caught fire. Taylor grabbed the frying pan, but it tilted and spilled. The blazing grease splashed his right hand and burned his right foot. He spent 10 days in the hospital with severe burns. Although he played only half the season, Taylor still gained 452 yards.

The Packers learned that Jim was something special in 1960 when he slammed through enemy lines for 1,101 yards and broke the Packer team record. In the championship game with the Philadelphia Eagles, Taylor carried the ball 25 times for 105 yards. With seconds to go, Taylor caught a pass and reached the Eagles' nine-yard line. But time ran out before the Packers could score, and Philadelphia won 17-13.

In 1961 Taylor scored 15 touchdowns and gained 1,307 yards, the most any player ever had gained, with the exception of Jim Brown. In the regular-season game against Cleveland, Taylor outshined Brown, scoring four touchdowns in a 49-17 Packer victory. Taylor made more yards in that game (158) than the entire Brown offense.

Taylor's battering tactics helped the Packers clinch the Western Title in a game with the New York Giants, but he suffered painful rib injuries in the game. When the same two clubs met for the championship at Green Bay, Taylor was used largely as a decoy while Hornung gained most of the yardage as the Packers routed the Giants 37-0.

Jim's biggest year was 1962, when he won the rushing title that Jim Brown had owned for five straight years. Taylor ripped the defenses for 19 touchdowns, still the NFL record for running scores, and carried 272 times for 1,474 yards. Green Bay beat the Giants again in the title game 16-7.

In early 1963 Jim was struck down with hepatitis, a liver disease. When the season started, he was still not in top form, but he was forced to carry the heavy load alone. His running partner, Paul Hornung, was serving a one-year suspension from the league. Still, Taylor gained 1,018 yards. In 1964 he gained 1,169 yards and became the only NFL player ever to gain 1,000 or more yards in five straight years.

There were whispers that Taylor had gone over the hill during the 1965 season when he limped through most of the regular season, unable to cut or drive off of his left foot. His Achilles tendon, the "lever" that works the foot, had been torn in the final preseason game. It was not until the December 12 game in Baltimore that the injury healed enough to permit Taylor to drive with his old power. Then he pulled a groin muscle in the Baltimore game and limped through the season finale and the play-off game with Baltimore.

In fact, Taylor was not able to run all week before the title game with Cleveland. There was doubt about his availability until the end of the week. Yet he won the Most Valuable Player award.

"You don't sit out this kind of a game," said Taylor as the trainer bandaged his left leg before the big game with the Browns. "Hurt or not, you play. You have all winter to rest."

As Lombardi said, Jim Taylor is a man who always rises to the occasion. That is what separates the men from the boys in pro football.

OLLIE MATSON chapter five

When sprinters Bob Hayes and Henry Carr decided to make the leap from the Olympics to pro football in 1965, they knew it could be done. Ollie Matson had shown them the way. Matson, a quarter-miler at the 1952 Olympics, proved that a track man can be durable enough to stand up under the strenuous work of professional football.

Many great track stars have failed in pro football because they could do nothing but run fast. Too many had no football background and tried to get by on speed alone. For example, Frank Budd, the fastest sprinter of his day, never learned to combine his speed with the disciplined patterns so necessary to a good pass receiver. He was soon dropped from pro ball. Many other track stars have tried and failed. Matson was one of the few to go to the top in both fields.

"When I broke in," Matson has said, "everybody used to tell me, 'You're not a football player. You're a track man. You're not built ruggedly enough.' That just made me try all the harder."

Matson had always tried hard. Barely out of high school in 1948, he ran the quarter mile in 47.4 seconds and the 100-yard dash in 9.7 seconds in an Amateur Athletic Union track meet. Despite his good performance, he missed winning a place on the United States Olympic team that year.

Four years later, after the Chicago (now St. Louis) Cardinals in the NFL had made him their first choice of all the college football players in the country, Ollie still remembered his Olympic ambitions. Before he signed a football contract, he was determined to make a place for himself on the United States Olympic team for the 1952 Games at Helsinki.

Although Ollie had not trained strenuously

Ollie Matson relaxes after qualifying for the 1952 U.S. Olympic Team in the 400-meter run.

for track for four years, he drove himself through a punishing series of conditioning tests. His college had no track team at the time, so he mapped out his own program and worked through the winter and early spring of 1952 to regain the rhythm and stamina he had in high school.

Matson's biggest race of the spring was against Herb McKenley of Jamaica (a small island country in the Caribbean Sea). McKenley held the world record for the quarter mile. Going into the last fifty yards, Ollie was still ahead. But McKenley called on his last ounce of strength and overtook Matson before reaching the finish line.

In the Olympic trials Matson ran second to George Rhoden, another Jamaican, who was studying in the United States. But Ollie qualified for the United States team and made the trip to Helsinki, Finland, that summer.

In a preliminary trial at Helsinki Ollie ran second again to Rhoden, who was competing for Jamaica. In the finals, Matson streaked home third in 46.8 seconds, finishing behind his two old adversaries, Rhoden and Herb McKenley, both competing for Jamaica.

In the 1,600-meter relay, the United States'

Matson breaks the tape in the 100-yard dash in the 1952 Drake Relays.

toughest competition came from the Jamaicans once again. Matson ran first opposite Arthur Wint, the Jamaican giant, and turned over a two-yard lead to America's second man, Gene Cole. On the third leg McKenley was clocked at an amazing 44.6 seconds and took the lead for Jamaica. Rhoden held Jamaica's slim lead on the anchor leg. Both the winning Jamaica team and the United States broke the world record in a photo finish. Jamaica was timed in 3 minutes, 3.9 seconds and the United States in 3 minutes, 4 seconds.

Dink Templeton, the Stanford University coach who helped Ollie get ready for the Olympics, said that if Matson had been running the quarter mile for three years, like the rest of the competitors, no one would have finished close to him.

Ollie's interest in track and football came naturally. He was born on May 1, 1930, at Trinity, Texas. His father was a railroad brakeman, and his mother was a schoolteacher. He began running in track meets before he reached high school, and his interest in football was sparked by an uncle, Theodore Haynes, who had been a semiprofessional player in Houston. When he was in junior high, Ollie told his mother, "I want to be like Uncle

Ted." He went out for football, but the coach told him he was "too small."

When Ollie was 15, the family moved to San Francisco. By then he was on his way to becoming the six-foot-two, 210-pounder of his future pro days and was no longer too small for football.

In his first game at San Francisco's George Washington High School, Ollie ran 56 yards for a touchdown. But on the next play he suffered a broken ankle and was out for most of the season. But in his senior year he attracted national attention by scoring 102 points in one season. The New York (football) Yankees of the All-America Conference had spotted Ollie and suggested that he turn professional. But Ollie knew he wasn't ready for the pros. He wanted to go to college.

He went to San Francisco City College for one semester, just long enough for the football season. His team had an undefeated season, and Ollie scored 19 touchdowns. Scholarship offers poured in from such major universities as Marquette, UCLA, Oregon and Ohio State. Ollie considered them but chose to stay near home and attend the University of San Franscico, a Roman Catholic men's college with approximately 3,500 students.

USF was on the way to becoming a football power under coach Joe Kuharich. The careers of Kuharich and Matson were to touch several times in the following years.

San Francisco opened the 1949 season against St. Bonaventure, then a small-college football power. The St. Bonaventure coach met Ollie on the sidelines before the game and made the mistake of belittling him and taunting him about his great reputation. Matson replied by breaking loose for two touchdowns in six minutes on runs of 92 and 42 yards. Later that season he ran 60 and 53 yards against Loyola of Los Angeles and 80 yards against San Jose State.

Matson reached the peak of his college career in 1951, his senior season. San Francisco had become a big football school in the West but was almost unknown in the East. Then Kuharich scheduled a game with Fordham in a New York stadium. Matson simply ran wild against the Rams. With the score tied at 19-19 he grabbed a kickoff and ran 90 yards down the sidelines for the touchdown. By the time the game was over, Matson had scored three touchdowns, made spectacular runs of 94 and 90 yards and gained 302 yards.

In his senior year, he led the nation in scoring with 21 touchdowns and in yards gained with 3,166. He was selected to All-America teams at two different positions — fullback and defensive safety — a tribute to his skill not only as a runner but as a pass defender.

"If Ollie had played football at Notre Dame he'd be known as another Jim Thorpe or Red Grange," said Joe Kuharich. "Ollie was the best all-around football player I've ever seen or coached. The three great backs I have seen in pro football were Ollie, Jim Brown and Marshall Goldberg. Ollie was so good that coaches sometimes were puzzled as to how he did it. No one could match his speed when he first came along, and he had as much power as any plunging fullback. In college he was Mr. Inside and Mr. Outside and just about Mr. Everything."

In the annual college draft, the Los Angeles Rams, who had the first bonus pick by lot, passed Ollie up and took Bill Wade, a quarterback who later became the regular signal-caller for the Chicago Bears. But unsurprisingly, the Cardinals, who had the next pick, chose the San Francisco speedster.

Before going to work for the Cardinals,

Matson went to the Olympics. Then he hurried home from the Olympics to report to the College All-Star team to get ready for the game with the NFL champion Rams. He was used as a defensive back and did a magnificent job of covering Elroy "Crazy Legs" Hirsch, one of the greatest pass receivers in football. When sports writers chose the game's most valuable player, Matson was second to Babe Parilli, the All-Star quarterback, a great achievement for a defensive player.

After a hectic summer, Ollie reported to the Cardinals' training camp at Lake Forest, Illinois. Joe Kuharich, his old college coach, had been named coach of the Cardinals and was starting his first season as a head coach in the pro league.

In college Ollie had carried the ball at arm's length, allowing him to pump both his arms to pick up speed. This worked in college, but it wouldn't work in the pro league. Those big defensive men would hit his arm and the ball would pop out. After an epidemic of fumbles, he learned to cradle the ball.

Matson's first game ended on a sour note — he was ejected from the game for fighting with Sammy Baugh. But his total of 36 yards led the

Cards in rushing.

The second game was against the Bears, the Cards' cross-town rivals. Matson had to do better this time. He took a kickoff on his own goal line and angled toward the sidelines. Following his blocking, he sped 100 yards for a touchdown. Later in the game he stole a ball from a Bear and rambled 30 yards for a second score. Later in the season, he put on another dazzling display by scoring three touchdowns within six minutes against Pittsburgh.

But he spent most of his rookie year learning pro football. He found out that the hip blocks he used in college were not enough to protect the Card passer from the rushing defensive lineman. He learned to get his shoulder and the weight of his whole body into the block. He also learned how to hold on to the ball and how to run recklessly to the inside without hesitation.

The Army took Matson in 1953, and he spent part of the year playing football at Fort Ord in California. When he returned to the Cardinals in 1954, Kuharich had been replaced as coach. But Ollie soon came into his own as the most feared runner on the Cardinal ball club.

In 1956 he had his greatest season, gaining 924 yards. He lost the rushing title to the Bears' Rick Casares who had gained 1,126 yards. Ollie would have won it if gains of 350 yards had not been called back for penalties. Matson was so fast that he often got in front of his interference, and the blockers would hit his pursuers from behind, causing a clipping penalty.

That was the closest Ollie ever came to winning a rushing title and also the closest to playing on a championship team. If the Cards had been able to pick up seven extra points in strategic games they would have won the Eastern Conference title. As it was, they finished second to the New York Giants.

Ollie never was an elusive broken-field runner; instead, he combined power with great speed. He was great on the pitch to the outside, and opposing coaches developed gray hair trying to set up a defense for him. There was only one solution — drive him to the inside. When Ollie faced a defensive back one-on-one, he was nearly impossible to stop.

"I always liked to run to the sidelines," he said. "When I get over there I can see everything.

*Ollie shows his power as he pulls away from Cleveland Brown
defenders in a 1957 San Francisco-Cleveland game.*

There is no blind spot. Then I can decide whether I
can outrun a defensive man or try to cut back and
avoid him. In the open field I could get caught
from behind while trying to maneuver. Those

tackles from behind are the worst."

Except for Matson, the Cardinal attack was almost nonexistent. "I wonder what it would have been like for him if he had been with a real football team," an opposing coach once said. If the Cards had had a topflight quarterback or another real running back, Matson's record might have equaled that of Jim Brown or Steve Van Buren.

When the Cards traded Ollie to Los Angeles

As a Los Angeles Ram, Matson churns through his old Forty-Niner teammates.

in 1959 for nine other players, the football world was stunned. "Nine men for one player. Who ever heard of such a thing?" they said.

George Halas, owner-coach of the Bears, was amazed that the Cardinals would trade him even for nine other men. "I don't know how you could trade him," said Halas. "He is a wonder player, and you just don't trade away wonder players. There isn't enough value that you can receive to make you give up on a fellow like that."

The Rams were prepared to sacrifice anything — even nine men — to win a championship. They were convinced that Matson would make the difference. With Matson and Jon Arnett running the ball and Bill Wade passing, how could they lose?

They finished with only two wins and ten losses. The great Ram plan had failed. As a result Ram coach Sid Gillman was replaced by Bob Waterfield.

It was fashionable to say that Matson failed with the Rams. It might have been more truthful to say that the Rams failed with Matson. During his first season, Matson had carried the ball for 863 yards from scrimmage and added enough yardage by pass receptions, punt runbacks and kickoff returns to total 1,421 yards. He was the Rams' top runner and finished third among the rushers in the league. He was also their best pass receiver, with 33 receptions for 465 yards. And he was the best kick-return man on the Rams or any other club, possibly the best in the long history of the league. In one game against the Bears he carried the ball 31 times and gained 199 yards. Both marks still rate among the top individual efforts in Ram history.

But Matson's stay with the Rams was not easy. He was bounced from position to position like a ping-pong ball. In 1960 Waterfield tried him as a defensive back after Dick Bass took over the fullback job. In 1961 Matson was a slot back used as the man-in-motion in Waterfield's new offense.

Disillusioned when he lost his slot back job and saw action only on the kickoff team, Ollie played out his option with the Rams in 1962. He planned to seek work with another team in 1963. Professional players may negotiate with other teams if they play one season after taking a cut in pay and refuse to sign a new contract.

Matson finally changed his mind and agreed to return to the Rams in 1963. The Rams had a new coach and Matson had a chance to win back his old fullback job. But then the Rams traded Ollie to the Detroit Lions before the season even started. The Lions used him as a tight end and as a substitute for fullback Nick Pietrosante until he was sidelined because of an injury.

In 1964 Joe Kuharich, his old college and pro coach, took over as head coach with the Philadelphia Eagles. One of Kuharich's first moves was to make a trade with Detroit for Matson.

Matson was delighted. "Back home," as he described it, he came back strong with the Eagles. Pressed into service as a running back when Timmy Brown suffered an injury, Ollie ran for 100 yards in 19 carries against New York and ran 54 yards for a touchdown. With Brown out of action for several weeks, Matson wound up the year with 404 yards in 96 carries and an average of 4.2 yards per carry.

Although he was used sparingly in 1965, Matson finished the season with a career total of 12,209 yards, or almost seven miles, in runs, pass receptions and kick runbacks. The only man with more total NFL yardage is Cleveland's Jim Brown. And the record books still list Matson's record of eight touchdowns on kickoff returns as the best in NFL history.

Ollie Matson is living proof that an Olympic track star can succeed in professional football. A big-leaguer since 1952, he has made a mark on the NFL.

BRONKO
NAGURSKI
chapter
six

Coach Steve Owen sat in the New York Giants' office on a cold Sunday evening in 1934. His Giants had just lost a football game to the Chicago Bears, and a room full of sports writers were badgering him with questions.

"Just how do you go about setting up a defense for a man like Bronko Nagurski?" one of them asked.

"Defense him?" roared Owen. "There is only one way to defense Nagurski — shoot him before he leaves the dressing room."

Bronko Nagurski was the Chicago Bears'

fullback who had already become a football legend. Like Paul Bunyan, the fabled lumber camp hero, Bronko came from Minnesota, and the stories about him are often bigger than life.

Nagurski himself is used to tall tales about himself. But when he was asked if he ever heard about the time he missed a wild tackle and sheared off the side of a model-T Ford parked on the sidelines, it was too much for even the Bronk to swallow.

"Gosh, I've heard some good ones," he said. "Like the time I was supposed to have run over a horse. But I don't think I ever heard that I tore up an automobile."

The Bronk, who weighted 232 pounds in his playing days, had a habit of slamming into a ball carrier with a tremendous body block instead of a tackle when he was playing defense. Often the ball would get away from the ball carrier, and almost always, he would be knocked clear off his feet.

Once in a game between Nagurski's Chicago Bears and the Green Bay Packers, Clark Hinkle, the Packer ball carrier, found a hole in the Bear line, just inside George Musso, a huge tackle. Nagurski, who was playing in the backfield, saw

Bronko Nagurski demonstrates his form during a Bears practice.

the play coming and threw his body block at Hinkle. Hinkle bounced back a few yards and then came through the hole again. Once more the Bronk hit him with a body block. Hinkle rebounded five yards back but managed to keep his feet. Then he churned through the hole and went all the way for a touchdown.

"That is the first time I ever saw a back go past me three times on the same play," said Musso.

Later in the game Nagurski broke over left tackle on the Packers' 35, trampled the defense and plunged over the goal line. But he had gained so much momentum that he slammed headfirst into the brick wall of the grandstand and knocked himself out. When trainer Andy Lotshaw's cold towels brought him around, his first question was, "Who hit me?"

Bronko played in the days when a football player worked the whole ball game. When the Bears had the ball, Nagurski was fullback. When the other teams had the ball, he was often a tackle. In those days, NFL teams had only 18 men on the squad and could not afford the luxury of specialists who played only on offense or defense. Despite the heavy workload, the salaries were low. Bronko never earned more than $5,000 a year during his

The Bronko side-steps a tackler.

nine years with the Bears.

Nagurski came too early to cash in on the high salaries and bonuses of modern pro football or to take advantage of being a specialist on offense or defense. "I could have played for 20 more years if we'd had the platoon system in those days," he said recently. "But we had a lot more fun. With squads of 18 men, we got to play football both ways. The way it is now a fellow sits on the bench too much. I wouldn't have liked that."

Nagurksi was born of Polish-Ukranian parents, in Canada, in a place called Rainy River, Ontario. His first name was Bronislau. The family moved to International Falls, Minnesota, when Bronislau was just a lad.

The first time his father took him to school, the teacher had trouble understanding Mr. Nagurski's thick accent. The best the teacher could make of the name Bronislau was "Bronko." So his dad let it go at that. His name was Bronko from then on, and Bronislau was forgotten.

Bronko's high school football team at International Falls didn't win a game. No scouts had come to watch Bronko play, and when he reported to Doc Spears, the head coach at the University of Minnesota, he was just another big strong 230-pound boy from the north country.

Spears was getting his varsity ready for a big game with Michigan and had set up a special off-tackle power play for his big fullback, Herb Joesting. He called on the freshmen to act as the defensive team in practice.

The varsity ran the first play at Bronko, who was one of the freshman tackles. The Bronk gathered the ball carrier in his arms and dumped him back for a five-yard loss. Again and again the varsity tried the same play with the same results. When Spears gave the freshman the ball, Nagurski stomped over linemen, brushed aside the secondary and rumbled in to the end zone.

"I've got a kid who is just about an All-America right now," Spears told the newspapermen before Bronko's sophomore year. "The only trouble is I don't know where to play him."

Spears started Nagurski at end, a position he always maintained was Bronko's natural position. But later he needed a tackle and so made his star end a lineman. Before Bronko finished his college career he played every position except center and halfback.

In his senior year, 1929, Nagurski was picked as a tackle for Grantland Rice's All-America team although he had played the position only 20 minutes during the Big Ten season. The New York *Daily News* picked him as its All-America fullback. When Rice was asked to compare Nagurski with the two other great football stars, Red Grange and Jim Thorpe, he said he believed that a team of eleven Nagurskis could have beaten eleven Granges or eleven Thorpes.

It did not take Bronko long to make the leap from college to professional ball. George Halas, owner-coach of the Chicago Bears, contacted him through mutual friends and invited him to Chicago. The Bronk finally agreed to play with Halas for $5,000 a year.

The 1930 Bears opened the season against the old football-playing Brooklyn Dodgers and then headed West for another game in their bitter rivalry with the Green Bay Packers.

Red Grange, Bronko's teammate, tells the story of that Bear-Packer game. Cal Hubbard, a huge Packer tackle, wanted to take a crack at Nagurski to see if he was really as tough as his reputation. He asked Grange to let him through on one play to test Nagurski. Hubbard slammed through the line and crashed into Nagurski. He hit and bounced — back. Hubbard picked himself off the ground and ran down the field toward Grange.

"That's enough," he told him. "He is just as tough as they said he was."

The Bears finished third in 1930 and again in 1931, but in 1932 they went all the way to the NFL title. In addition to his running prowess, Nagurski now had developed a sideline. He occasionally threw a pass. In the 1932 championship game with

Portsmouth, Ohio, (later the Detroit Lions), Nagurski slammed toward the line and then quickly dropped back and flipped a short touchdown pass to Red Grange. Nagurski's jump pass turned out to be a most important weapon for the Bears in succeeding years as the game of pro football became a wide-open, freewheeling spectacular.

With Nagurski ripping through enemy lines with those powerful legs on offense and throwing his mammoth body against ball carriers on defense, the Bears won Western Division titles in 1933, 1934 and 1937. In '33 they beat the New York Giants for the league crown and in 1934 they lost a heartbreaker to the Giants on an icy field in New York. The Giants won the game by changing from football cleats to sneakers for the second half. Since the sneakers made the footing easier for the Giants, they outmaneuvered the Bears and won 30-13.

Arthritis and the aches and pains of a thousand jolting collisions finally took their toll on Nagurski in 1935, and he no longer was the powerful fullback and 60-minute man of yore. An operation for removal of a bone spur from his hip sidelined him for part of the season. Contract

Bronko charges toward the New York Giant line in the 1934 championship game. The Bear quarter-back waits to hand off the ball to the Bronk.

Nagurski carries two Giant tacklers with him toward the goal in the 1934 championship game.

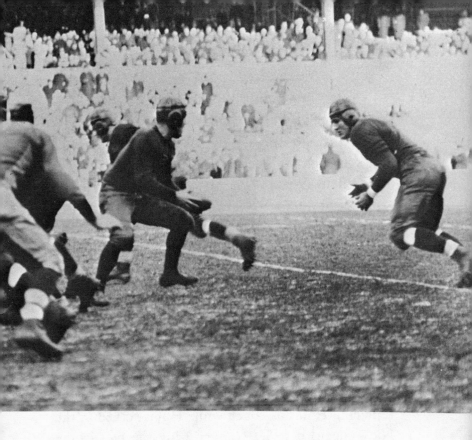

arguments with the Bears and persistent physical troubles finally led to Bronko's retirement after the 1937 season but not before the Bears had won another division title.

Despite his aches and pains, Nagurski had become a professional wrestler in 1934. In one three-week span in 1937, he played five football games with the Bears and wrestled in such widely separated cities as Duluth, Portland, Vancouver, Seattle, Phoenix, Los Angeles, Salt Lake City and

Philadelphia. After he quit football, he devoted all his time to wrestling. He worked every night and twice claimed the world championship.

When World War II came along and the younger players were called into the service, Halas talked Nagurski into making a comeback with the Bears in 1943. Though Bronko was 35, he still played with his old fire and drive.

"That Nagurski is really something," said his old pal, George Musso. "He's an old man and he can hardly walk but he knocks over those kids like a strong young kid just out of high school."

The Bears used Bronko only as a tackle during much of the season. But Hunk Anderson, who was replacing Halas as coach while Halas served in the Navy, decided to let Nagurski lug the ball in the game against the Chicago (now St. Louis) Cardinals. With the ball on the Cards' 38 and the Bears in need of a score, Nagurski slammed into the line seven straight times for the touchdown that wrapped up a 35-24 victory.

When the Bears met the Washington Redskins in the 1943 championship game, it was Nagurski's three-yard plunge that broke a 7-7 tie and put the Bears out front at the half. Washington prevailed

Nagurski was also a champion wrestler.

in the second half on Sammy Baugh's passing and won the game.

Nagurski's ground-gaining figures are not complete because the league maintained only sketchy statistics in the early days. But available figures show he carried the ball 872 times and gained 4,031 yards, an average of 4.6 yards per carry. In addition, he completed 38 of 80 passes, not bad for a fullback.

The Bronk now lives in his home town of

International Falls, Minnesota. He spends most of his spare time hunting and fishing for walleyed pike but does see an occasional NFL game at Minnesota, Green Bay or Chicago.

Nagurski's career is one of the greatest examples of all-around football. His records as a runner have been broken, and many feel that there have been one or two fullbacks even better than he was. But those who watched him play still believe that eleven Nagurskis would probably beat eleven of anyone else — even eleven Jimmy Browns.

PAUL
HORNUNG
chapter
seven

Vince Lombardi squirmed in his office chair as he watched the films of the 1958 Green Bay Packers. It was almost a horror movie. The Packers had struggled through a miserable season, winning only once in twelve games. Not since 1919 had the team finished with such a sorry record.

Alarmed by this disastrous tailspin, the Packers' directors had hired Lombardi from the New York Giants. As an assistant coach in New York, Lombardi had been credited with developing the Giants' offense.

Suddenly he shouted, "Let's see that again."

The man at the projector ran the film backward and then ran the play again. Across the silver screen came the image of Paul Hornung, taking a hand-off from Bart Starr. Hornung started wide around right end and then cut back quickly. It reminded Lombardi of the way Frank Gifford of the Giants made the same maneuver.

"The more I looked at Hornung in the movies, the more I figured he was the fellow I was looking for," said Lombardi. "He was bigger and could run harder than Gifford, but he still didn't have Giff's moves."

Hornung had been less than sensational in his two years as a pro. The Packers, who had selected him as their bonus choice draftee in 1957, were having second doubts. "Golden Dome," "Bonus Plum" and "Goat Shoulders" were some of the unflattering names the Packers fans had pinned on the former All-America quarterback from Notre Dame.

It was a far cry from the day when he went from Flaget High School in Louisville to Notre Dame University with the words of Notre Dame coach Frank Leahy ringing in his ears. "Paul Hornung will be the greatest quarterback Notre

Paul Hornung catches his breath during a tough game.

Dame has ever had," said Leahy. "He runs like a mower going through grass. Tacklers just fall off him. He can punt 80 yards and place-kick over the crossbar from 70 yards out."

But it wasn't that easy. Leahy left Notre Dame after Hornung's freshman year. With Ralph Guglielmi firmly entrenched as the number-one quarterback, the new coach, Terry Brennan, used Paul at fullback in his sophomore year. After Guglielmi graduated, Hornung took over as first-string quarterback. He could run and he could throw but he also could be intercepted. "Paul has got to improve on his passing," warned coach Brennan.

Notre Dame had a sad team in 1956, Paul's senior year. They won only two games. It was strictly a one-man effort. Hornung finished second in the nation in total yards gained with 1,337. Against Southern California he ran back a kickoff 95 yards. And against Michigan State he made 10 tackles as a defensive star. Despite his team's poor record and a few of his own bad moments, Paul had almost lived up to Coach Leahy's boasts. He was chosen on nearly every All-America team and was awarded the Heisman Trophy — as the best college football player in the country.

The Packers used their bonus choice in the annual draft to select Hornung. Lisle Blackbourn, then Packer head coach, was enthusiastic about Hornung. "He has a great potential," he raved. "He should be the greatest passer in the league." But when Blackbourn got a close-up look at Hornung, he changed his mind. In one sad performance as starting quarterback against the New York Giants in an exhibition game, Hornung had to be benched.

Blackbourn decided that Hornung couldn't throw the ball accurately enough to be a quarterback. He decided he couldn't run fast enough to be a halfback. He figured he didn't have the power to be a pro fullback. So he used him in all three positions. Hornung was the Packers' second best ground gainer. But he was unhappy.

Between seasons, Coach Blackbourn lost his job to Scooter McLean. Hornung's second year in pro ball under coach McLean was happier than the first but not too successful from the point of accomplishment. As a part-time fullback, he had led the Packers in running and scoring but was thinking of quitting pro ball.

Then Vince Lombardi became the Packer coach. Hornung was at home in Louisville when he read a quote from Lombardi one day in a newspaper. "Let's face it," Lombardi had told the reporter. "Hornung is the guy who can make us go. We'll see what he can do as a pass-run option halfback. Much will depend on how quickly he can decide whether to run or pass."

Paul was quick to see the change in the climate when he reported for the Packer training season. Lombardi was strictly business. "I've never been a losing coach and I don't intend to start," he told the team.

At the first practice session Lombardi called Hornung to the sidelines. "You are going to be my left halfback," Lombardi told Hornung. "Either you play left half or you don't play. You are going to sink or swim at that position."

Hornung was satisfied. For the first time in his pro career he was going to get a chance to play regularly. He knew how important the left halfback was in Lombardi's scheme of attack. Although the quarterback remained key man in Lombardi's T formation, the left half really carried the heavy load. He had to run the ball, catch passes and block. Most important of all, he had to make that pass-option play go. He would take a hand-off or a pitchout and start driving wide. Then in a split second he had to decide whether to keep on running or stop quickly and fire a pass. In time Hornung became every bit as good as the Giants' Frank Gifford, who nearly created the play.

With Hornung at left half and Jim Taylor at fullback, the Packers began to move. They finished the 1959 season with a 7-5 record, placing third in the Western Conference, only two games behind the champion Baltimore Colts.

Lombardi was on the way and so was Hornung. The fans weren't calling Paul unflattering names any more. Hornung had led the league in scoring, with 94 points on seven touchdowns, 31 conversions and seven field goals. He had led the Packers in rushing with 681 yards on 152 carries and had caught 15 passes for 113 yards. Running the old Gifford-type option, Hornung had thrown eight passes and completed five for 95 yards and two big touchdowns.

The Golden Boy really came into his own in 1960 when the Packers won the Western Conference title with an 8-4 record. The fun-loving Hornung, with his curly blond hair and dimpled cheek, caught the fancy of the fans and the writers.

During his first big season (1960), Hornung squirms away from three Balitmore tacklers.

He set a record that still stands by scoring 176 points. He ran for 13 touchdowns, caught two touchdown passes, kicked 41 straight conversions and made good with 15 of 28 field-goal attempts. He also threw two touchdown passes.

Only the failure of the Packers in the title game with Philadelphia marred the fine season. The Packers lost 17-13, and Paul suffered a neck injury in the third period. The game ended with the Packers deep in Eagle territory, lacking only the time to score.

The loss of the championship only made the Packers more determined to go all the way in 1961. Hornung had the biggest day of his career in the fourth week of the 1961 season against Baltimore. With Jerry Kramer, Fuzzy Thurston and Jim Taylor running interference, Paul ran 54 yards for the first touchdown and kicked the extra point. Then he kicked a field goal. Later he plunged over the goal from point-blank range and added a second extra point. At half time it was 17-7, and Hornung had scored all the Green Bay points.

Bart Starr hit Hornung with a scoring pass in the third period, and a few minutes later Paul swept 10 yards, breaking tackles as he ran, for his

Fuzzy Thurston leads the way, Hornung carries the ball.

fourth touchdown. He kicked the conversions after each touchdown. He added two more extra points in the fourth period and wound up with a total of 33 points, a Packer record.

The following week at Cleveland, Hornung did the blocking and Jim Taylor carried the ball, scoring four touchdowns. Those two resounding victories, 45-7 and 49-17, were the high points of a championship year. In fact, Lombardi has said that the Cleveland game was the all-time peak for his Packer teams.

Hornung was called into the Army in midseason and was stationed at Fort Riley in Kansas. When he was able to get weekend passes, a Green Bay citizen flew him in his private plane from Kansas to the town where the Packers were playing. Paul missed three games altogether, but he still led the league in scoring for the third straight season with 146 points.

Luckily, Hornung received a short leave before the Packers' championship game against the New York Giants. He had had trouble with his timing during his week-long absences during the season, but he was able to pick up the threads when he returned for 10 days of practice.

It was the first time a title game had ever been played in Green Bay, and the city was plastered with signs that proclaimed the site as "Titletown USA." Hornung ran the Giants dizzy, and the Packers won 37-0. Paul's total of 19 points set an all-time record for championship games. He scored one touchdown, kicked four extra points and added three field goals. This game and the early season contest with Baltimore showed Hornung at his very best.

The Army released Hornung just in time for the 1962 training season, but he suffered an injury to his right knee in an early game and carried the ball only 57 times all season. Despite his limited service, Paul scored 74 points. They were not enough to give him a fourth straight scoring title. His teammate Jim Taylor won it with 114 points.

Commissioner Pete Rozelle suspended Hornung for the entire 1963 season for violating the NFL rule that prohibits players from betting on the outcome of games. A penitent Hornung admitted, "I made a terrible mistake. I am truly sorry that I did wrong. I should be penalized."

Hornung was reinstated for the 1964 season and drove himself through a rigorous training routine. He knew everybody would be watching to see if he could come back after an absence of a full year. He reported to Green Bay late in the spring. Day after day he ran up and down the 60 concrete steps in the stadium, building up his leg muscles and testing his damaged knee. When the season started he was in midseason form.

But something was wrong. The Packers were having trouble keeping up with the Chicago Bears. And Hornung had suddenly lost his touch as a

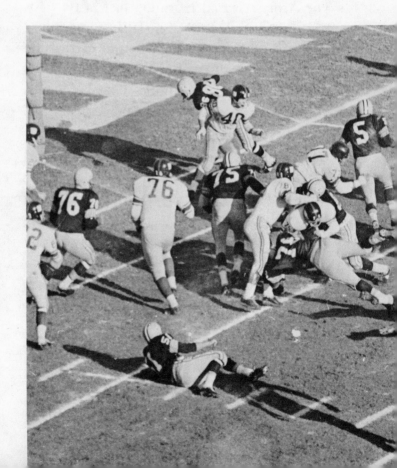

kicker. The old dependable place kicker of the other years couldn't find the range. Against Baltimore he missed five straight field goals. In another game he missed an extra point that meant the difference between a tie and a costly defeat. Although he scored 107 points, Hornung had a shockingly poor record at kicking, making only 12 of 38 attempted field goals.

Through it all, Hornung never lost his sense of humor. When a reporter asked him about the

Hornung (5) scores against the Giants in the 1961 title game. He also kicked three extra points and three field goals.

season, he shrugged his shoulders and grinned as he punned, "I can't kick."

After the 1964 season Lombardi traded with the Giants for Don Chandler, a superior place kicker. Although the coach kept saying that Hornung also would do some kicking, he never did. Chandler took over, and Hornung became strictly a ball carrier.

Riding the bench was a new experience to Paul. He had started every game since Lombardi became coach, with the exception of those he missed because of Army duty or injury. In 1965 Lombardi let him sit out three games. There were times when a pulled hamstring muscle bothered him. But there also were times when he felt healthy but just didn't play.

When the Packers came to Baltimore to play a crucial game with the Colts, December 12, Hornung got his chance. Lombardi decided it was time to switch back to his veterans. After drilling the team in privacy at a secluded motel near Washington, Lombardi announced, "Hornung will be my left halfback. He always rises to the occasion."

Hornung's performance proved Lombardi's

Paul leaps across the goal line for another touchdown.

statement. By the time the Colts dragged themselves off the field, Hornung had scored five touchdowns, the biggest explosion of his career. If he still had been kicking extra points and field

Covered with mud from head to toe, Hornung carries a short gain against Cleveland in the 1965 Championship game.

goals he would have surpassed his record of 33 points in one game. Paul scored on runs of 2, 9 and 3 yards and caught scoring passes of 50 and 65 yards from Bart Starr. He gained 61 yards on 15 carries and 115 yards on two pass catches. The Packers won 42-27.

In the final game of the season, the Packers tied with San Francisco, 24-24, making a Packers-Colts playoff game necessary to determine the Western Conference winner. Although he had a battered knee, a swollen wrist and a painfully bruised chest, Hornung scored the only touchdown against the Colts in·a game won on a Chandler field goal, 13-10.

Now Green Bay faced the Cleveland Browns in the NFL championship game. The fans knew that Hornung and Taylor, the old pros, would rise to the occasion if the Packer defensive unit could hold Jimmy Brown, Cleveland's record-breaking fullback.

The defense held, and Hornung and Taylor came through. Hornung carried 18 times for 105 yards, including a 13-yard touchdown run and another brilliant 34-yard gallop. Workhorse Taylor was voted the Most Valuable Player award, but he shared the headlines with Hornung. It was an inspiring performance by the two old-timers who were to be challenged in 1966 by two high-priced young rookies, Donny Anderson of Texas Tech and Jim Grabowski of Illinois.

"I guess there's a little spark left in Paul and Jimmy," said Lombardi with a grin after the game.

"Just a couple of old-timers trying to hang on," chorused Hornung and Taylor.

Notre Dame coach Frank Leahy had predicted that Hornung would become Notre Dame's greatest quarterback. What he couldn't see was that Paul would become the greatest halfback the Green Bay Packers had ever had. Still, Paul's greatest talent is not his power or his speed. As Vince Lombardi has said, Hornung "smells that goal line."

JOE PERRY and HUGH McELHENNY
chapter eight

"Perry is like a bowling ball fired from a howitzer. It whistles down the middle of the alley and sends the pins flying in every direction.

"McElhenny is like a bowling ball thrown with 'body English.' It slides crazily down the alley, curls around the pins and scatters them gently.

"The result is essentially the same — a strike either way."

That was the way Frankie Albert, the great left-handed quarterback and coach of the San Francisco Forty-Niners, once described his old teammates Joe Perry and Hugh McElhenny.

Albert ran the team from the huddle or the bench during the seasons when Perry and McElhenny were setting records in San Francisco. The two of them — Perry a bruising fullback and McElhenny a swift halfback — made up one of the most explosive combinations ever seen in the National Football League.

Joe Perry was a stocky five-foot ten-inch, 208-pounder who learned his football at Jordan High School in Los Angeles, Compton (California) Junior College and the Alameda Naval Air Station.

In high school, Joe had to sneak away from home to go out for the team. "My mother didn't want me to play football," he recalls, "but I forged her name on the form giving permission. Wouldn't you know, I broke my ankle on the first day. I walked the three blocks home on that broken ankle, trying to hide it from her.

"But it swelled up and the pain got so bad I had to tell her. She said, 'Well, if you want to break your neck, go ahead.' After that she was my most enthusiastic fan."

Joe also excelled at track in high school. He

Joe Perry (above) and Hugh McElhenny (below) carry the ball for the Forty-Niners

ran the 100-yard dash in 9.7 seconds and was clocked at 21.9 seconds in the 220. After graduation from high school, he enrolled at nearby Compton Junior College. During one season at Compton he scored 22 touchdowns. Soon afterward he joined the Navy and began playing with the Alameda Naval Air Station team.

Perry's exploits on the Naval Air Station team first attracted the attention of the pro scouts.

John Woudenberg, Perry's Naval coach said of him, "Our offense is very simple. When we need to score we just give the ball to Joe Perry, point him in the right direction and step aside."

Soon Buck Shaw, coach of the San Francisco Forty-Niners in the old All-America Conference (a rival pro league that later merged with the NFL) practically lived at the field. After scouting Perry himself, Tony Morabito, owner of the Forty-Niners, offered him a contract as a free agent. Perry is one of the few men who became a pro star without playing first for a university team.

"Actually, the Los Angeles Rams offered me almost twice as much money," said Perry. "But I signed with the Forty-Niners because of Tony Morabito. I idolized that man. Actually, I never did sign a paper. A handshake with Tony always was good enough for me."

At about the same time, Perry was offered a baseball contract with the Oakland Oaks of the Pacific Coast League. Although the Oaks gave him permission to quit the club in time to join the Forty-Niners' training camp, he eventually decided against trying to excel in two professional sports in the same year.

In 1948, Joe's first year with San Francisco, he cut loose for an exciting 58-yard touchdown run against the Buffalo Bills. But then a torn knee cartilage put him out of action for the rest of the season. Still, he gained 1,345 yards in two seasons before the Forty-Niners merged with the NFL.

Perry wasn't all pure power and speed. He was a calculating student of football. Shaw once said, "Joe is the only man I ever saw who could sit down after a ball game and diagram the opposition's defense."

In 1949 quarterback Frankie Albert said of Perry, "When this guy comes past you to take the hand-off, the slip stream just about knocks you over. I'm telling you, he's jet-propelled."

The Forty-Niners joined the NFL in 1950. In

both of the next two seasons Perry finished fifth in the League in rushing statistics. In 1952 he placed third. Joe had come up the hard way, joining the club as a free agent without publicity and proving himself slowly. Things were different with Hugh McElhenny.

McElhenny had come from a Los Angeles high school like Perry. But after graduating from Washington High, he went north to the University of Washington and became one of the great stars of West Coast college football. He was named to most All-America teams and was the Forty-Niners' first pick in the college draft for the 1952 season.

Hugh was fresh from the College All-Star Game at Chicago when he checked in with the Forty-Niners. The team was getting ready to play its first exhibition. San Francisco fans still talk about McElhenny's first pro appearance in an exhibition game about two days after he reported back to camp.

Between plays, quarterback Albert trotted over to the sidelines and shouted, "Hey, coach, send in McElhenny."

McElhenny shakes loose one last tackler and heads for a touchdown against the Detroit Lions.

"I can't," Shaw replied. "He doesn't know the plays."

But Albert insisted. McElhenny came in, and Albert improvised a play on the palm of his hand in the huddle. It was a pitchout to McElhenny.

Hugh took the ball and went 40 yards to score.

Y. A. Tittle replaced Frankie Albert as first-string quarterback in 1953, and the Forty-Niners were beginning to roll. Perry won the rushing championship with 1,018 yards on 192 carries and scored 10 touchdowns. With his knees pumping high, McElhenny was making the spectacular runs that made him the darling of the fans.

McElhenny was always self-confident and became impatient when he thought others were making mistakes. In one game in 1953 McElhenny came back to the huddle after a fruitless run downfield on a pass play and complained to Tittle, "Y. A., hold it up a minute. Give us time to get out there and see how the secondary is setting up and what they are trying to do to defense us."

Tittle took one look at McElhenny. "If you don't like it, get out of here and get somebody else in," he barked.

McElhenny took Tittle at his word and trotted off the field. The amazed Coach Shaw sent him back in again on the next play.

Tittle and McElhenny later became the closest of friends. When Hugh was traded to the New York Giants in 1963, there was a joyful reunion between him and Y. A., who had been the regular Giant quarterback for several seasons.

"There never was an open-field runner like McElhenny," Tittle has said. "He was the finest running back I ever saw. He and Perry were a great combination. Joe ran like he was shot out of a cannon. The two of them made old Y. A. look pretty good for a lot of years."

With Perry and McElhenny approaching their peaks, the Forty-Niners presented an awesome attack in 1953 and 1954. Joe followed up his 1953 rushing title with another in 1954 when he became the first man ever to gain more than 1,000 yards two years in a row. He had gained 1,018 yards in 1953 and 1,049 in 1954. The mark stood until Jim Brown broke it after the NFL had increased its seasons to fourteen games. Teams played only 12 games in Joe's two title years.

By 1954 the combination of Perry, McElhenny, Tittle and John Henry Johnson was called the "Million Dollar Backfield." Although McElhenny suffered a shoulder separation and missed almost half the season, he still finished among the top 10 ground gainers, and Joe was jolting along stronger than ever.

Perry had learned to follow the advice of Coach Shaw and was able to maneuver his way around a defender instead of trying to run over him. "Joe had such tremendous speed that he used to run straight at a man as fast as he could," said

Surrounded by Bear tacklers,
Joe Perry drives forward for
an extra yard.

Shaw. "If one man got in his way he usually brought him down. It took time to get him to dodge, but once he learned there was no stopping him."

Despite their strong attack the Forty-Niners

won less than half their games in 1955 and 1956. Both Perry and McElhenny were troubled by injuries.

In 1957 the Forty-Niners almost went all the way. They finished the season in a tie for the Western Conference championship with the Detroit Lions. In the playoff game to decide the championship, the Forty-Niners had a 27-7 lead at half time. It looked as if they had their first conference title and a shot at the NFL championship. But the Lions came back in the second half with 27 points and beat the Forty-Niners 31-27.

The near-miss in 1957 marked the beginning of the end for the two great runners at San Francisco. The San Francisco management was in the mood for change. After two even less successful seasons head coach Frankie Albert was succeeded in 1959 by Red Hickey. In 1960 Perry lost his fullback job to J. D. Smith, and McElhenny, after gaining 128 yards in nine carries against the Chicago Bears, was used sparingly the rest of the season.

After the 1960 season the Forty-Niners traded McElhenny to the newly organized Minnesota Vikings. Durable Joe Perry was shuttled off to the

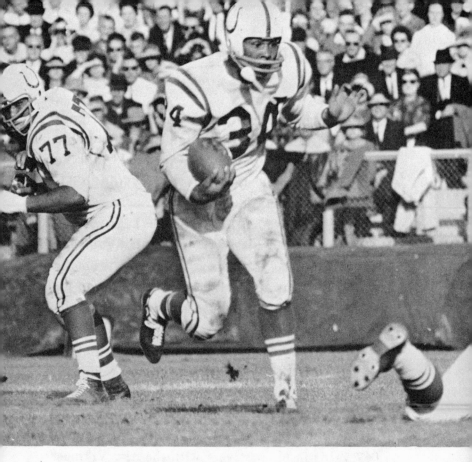

Still driving, Perry gains yards for the Colts in 1962.

Baltimore Colts, and Tittle was traded to the New York Giants.

After a career in which he had 30 stitches taken in his face, suffered 10 broken ribs and two shoulder separations and badly sprained an ankle at least 15 times, Perry still managed to lead Baltimore in rushing, with 675 yards in 1961. He also caught 34 passes for 322 yards. A torn knee ligament suffered in an exhibition game moved Joe close to the end of the trail in 1962. Still he outgained the great Jim Brown, 57 yards to 11, when the Colts met Cleveland.

Perry was traded back to San Francisco in 1963 and finished his career there. He gained a grand total of 8,378 yards in his 16 years in the NFL, ranking second only to Jim Brown. And his NFL totals do not include the 1,345 yards he gained in the All-America Conference.

McElhenny, who called himself "a thinking man's runner," thrived in the Minnesota climate. Working for Coach Norm Van Brocklin, he became the leader of a club made up of aging veterans and promising youngsters. He gained 1,067 yards in his first year with the new Vikings. Van Brocklin used him as a running back, a pass receiver, and as a punt and kick-return man. He excelled in all fields and called his 1961 season the best of his career.

A bad knee hobbled McElhenny in 1962, but he still gained 594 yards. But the Vikings were still building and traded McElhenny to the New York Giants to make room for younger players. The trade offered McElhenny the last hope of playing for a championship team. The Giants had won the Eastern Conference title in both 1961 and 1962 with Tittle calling the signals. They were favored again in 1963. Perhaps this would be the year when dreams of a championship would come true for both Hugh and Y.A.

At the Giants' camp in Fairfield, Connecticut, an astonished McElhenny could only stare in

In his last bid for a chance to play in a championship game, McElhenny helps the Giants beat the Cleveland Browns in the crucial game of the 1963 season.

surprise when his new coach, Allie Sherman, asked, "Are you ready to scrimmage?"

"That was the first time anybody ever asked me if I was ready in my life," he said later. "The others just told me what I was to do."

McElhenny was 34 when he reported to the Giants. He had injured his knee the previous season, and he had only remnants of his old artistry. But he still had that intense desire and pride. Although Mac's knee would not permit him to make the cuts with his old devastating speed, he was able to high step his way for 476 yards in 1963. In one game with Cleveland he earned his season's pay, helping the Giants to an all-important win on their way to a third straight Eastern crown.

Tears streamed down McElhenny's face when the Giant fans counted off the seconds — "Five, four, three, two, one," — as the club clinched the division title by beating Pittsburgh in the last game of the season. At last McElhenny and Tittle were going to get into a championship game.

"All those years at San Francisco when I was going good," said McElhenny, "we never made it. Now I'm finally in it at the tail end of my career. I'll give everything I have to help the Giants win."

But it was not in the cards for the Giants to win that cold, blustery afternoon at Wrigley Field. A rolling block by Larry Morris tore apart Tittle's knee in the first half, hobbling the Giants passing attack. McElhenny showed flashes of his old form but it wasn't enough. The Giants lost, and both Tittle and McElhenny had missed their last chance.

The following August, the Turk, that mythical figure who brings the bad news to washed-up veterans, knocked on McElhenny's door. "Allie wants to see you in his office," a Giant hired hand said.

"I'm going with younger boys," Sherman told him. "A lot of people probably won't understand the moves I am making but that is the way it has to be. Is there any way I can help you?"

McElhenny played a few games for the Detroit Lions in 1964, but he didn't have the old spark. He retired at the end of the season.

Although Perry and McElhenny are both retired, they still run in the record books. McElhenny's total yardage on rushing, pass catches, and kick returns adds up to 11,375 yards. Only Jim Brown and Ollie Matson have gained more. His average gain per carry of 10.69 yards in

1952 is still the second highest in league history. Joe Perry still ranks second only to Jim Brown in rushing yardage.

When sports fans talk of the great one-two combinations in professional football, many still claim that Joe Perry and Hugh McElhenny were the very best. As Tittle said, "They were the two greatest running backs who ever played for the same club."

ERNIE
NEVERS
chapter
nine

In the NFL Record Manual there appears the following entry: "Most Points One Game — 40, Ernie Nevers, Chicago Cardinals *vs.* Chicago Bears, Nov. 28, 1929 (6 touchdowns, 4 points-after-touchdown).

That one short entry tells a thousand words about fullback Ernie Nevers, who is among the very best running backs in the history of the NFL. Few NFL records have survived more than a few years, but Ernie's scoring record remains on the books nearly 40 years later.

To make his feat even more amazing, Ernie

scored his forty points in the days when final scores of 0-0 and 3-0 were common in professional football. They played a tough brand of football then. The forward pass was seldom used, and no pass receiver ever caught 15 or 18 passes per game as they do today. The accent was on the bruising, back-breaking running game.

Nevers' amazing record had been all but forgotten until Gale Sayers of the Chicago Bears scored six touchdowns in one game in 1965. When the press-box historians checked the record they found to their amazement that an old-timer named Nevers had once scored six touchdowns *and* kicked four extra points in the same game.

It was a cold and dreary Thanksgiving Day morning when the Cardinals and the Bears met for the 1929 Chicago city championship. There was a bitter rivalry between the two teams since they were fighting for the attendance of the Chicago fans as well as for victory. The Bears had always dominated the series, and their star Red Grange was a celebrity in Chicago. The Bears were heavily favored to win again. About 8,000 fans turned out for the game which was played in Comiskey Park. Comiskey was on the South Side of Chicago, the

Ernie Nevers at Stanford

"home territory" of the Cardinals (and of base-ball's White Sox). The crowd favored the Cardi-nals although past experience told them that the Bears had a better chance. The Cards hadn't beaten the Bears since 1927. Earlier in 1929 the best they could do was hold the Bears to a 0-0 tie.

When Nevers churned through the Bear defenses for a touchdown in the first six minutes of play, the crowd went wild. Ernie missed the extra point attempt with a wide kick. But minutes later he scored a second touchdown. This time he didn't miss the extra point, and the Cards led 13-0.

Before the first half was over Nevers had scored again and the score was 20-0. The Bears finally broke the shutout on a touchdown pass by Garland Grange, Red Grange's brother, but the Bears couldn't stop Nevers.

Three times in the second half Nevers slashed through that Bear line for touchdowns, and twice he made his extra-point attempt. The Cardinals had won easily, and Ernie left the field with five minutes to play in the final quarter. He received a tremendous ovation from the frenzied South Side fans.

Knute Rockne, the famous Notre Dame coach, sat in the stands, surrounded by the Notre

Dame team which came to Chicago from South Bend, Indiana, for the game. Rockne seldom smiled, but when Nevers scored his last touchdown Rockne's face lit up. He turned to his players and said, "That, gentlemen, is how to play football."

Rockne's admiration for Nevers dated back to the Rose Bowl Game of January 1, 1925. The legendary coach had brought one of his best teams to Pasadena, California, to play Nevers and the Stanford team. The Notre Dame backfield — Layton, Crowley, Stuhldreher and Miller — had become nationally famous as "The Four Horsemen."

Nevers had been a doubtful starter against Notre Dame. In a preseason scrimmage Ernie's left ankle had been broken when his cleats caught in the turf just as a tackler hit him. He missed most of the season but got back into action in the next to last game against Montana. Early in that game, a Montana lineman fell heavily on Nevers' other ankle, and it broke.

Although Nevers' ankle still was in a cast 10 days before the game, he convinced his coach, Pop Warner, that he could play. With his legs heavily bandaged and his ankles taped, Nevers hobbled out to face the mighty Four Horsemen.

Nevers played the entire game and put on one of the greatest performances ever seen in a Rose Bowl Game. One reporter wrote, "Nobody ever saw anybody exhibit greater skill than Nevers against Notre Dame. Not only did he stand out as a magnificent line-smashing fullback but he threw spiral passes, fast and true. He appeared to make four out of every five tackles on defense and intercepted a pass that started Stanford toward a touchdown."

Although Stanford lost 27-10, Nevers outgained the entire Four Horsemen backfield, carrying the ball 34 times for 114 yards. It was hard to believe that both his ankles had been broken earlier in the season.

Nevers' coach at Stanford, Pop Warner, had also coached the great Jim Thorpe. Thorpe was considered by many fans and writers to be the greatest football player ever. But when a writer asked Warner which player he thought was the greatest he had coached, Warner replied, "Ernie Nevers. Yes, better than Thorpe. Nevers could do everything Thorpe could do, and he always was trying harder than Thorpe ever did. Ernie gave everything in every game, but I rarely could get more than 15 or 20 minutes out of Thorpe. Ernie could hit his top running speed in two steps and could cut back or slice through an opening in the twinkling of an eye. He always went all out for me at Stanford, and he did the same thing later for the professionals. Yes, I'd have to say Nevers was better than Thorpe."

Nevers was born in Willow River, Minnesota, on June 11, 1903. When he was still a boy his family moved to Superior, Wisconsin. It was at Superior High School that he first began to attract attention as an athlete. When he first came out for football the coach used him as tackling dummy. Ernie would stand in a sawdust pit and the varsity players would try to tackle him. It didn't take long to convince the coach that Nevers belonged on the other side of the fence.

In basketball he developed a shot which may have become the basis for the game's first hook shot. He was so valuable in basketball that when his family moved to Santa Rosa, California, during his senior year, he got permission to return to Superior to play basketball after playing football for Santa Rosa High School.

At Stanford Nevers was one of the great basketball players in the school's history. He also pitched for the Stanford baseball team, and hit .400. He even took an occasional turn at throwing the discus for the track team when the baseball coach wasn't looking.

Pop Warner became Stanford football coach in Ernie's junior year. Warner installed the double wing attack and selected Nevers as the tailback — the man on whom the attack depended.

Nevers polished up his kicking and passing and became a real triple threat — he could run, pass or kick with equal skill. Unfortunately, that was the year he suffered the two broken ankles. But Stanford did advance all the way to the Rose Bowl.

Nevers was picked to several All-America teams in his senior year, 1925. Right after the football season he left Stanford to accept generous offers from the professionals. That winter Nevers was guaranteed $20,000 to play a series of exhibition games with an all-star team led by Red Grange.

Ernie then accepted a baseball offer from the St. Louis Browns in the American League. He received a bonus of $10,000 and a salary of $7,000 for the season. The Browns were a second division team and even Nevers didn't help them much. He appeared in only twelve games, winning two and losing four.

For the 1926 season, Ole Haugsrud, owner of the Duluth Eskimos of the NFL, offered him the position of player-coach at a salary of $20,000. Ernie also played a few pro basketball games with a Chicago team. Altogether, he earned about $60,000 in his first year as a pro in three sports.

The Eskimos played all their games on the road. They played 13 league games and padded the treasury by scheduling exhibition games wherever possible. In 1926 Duluth played 27 games, winning 17, losing seven and tying three.

The going with the Eskimos was rough. During one stretch in October they played five games in eight days. They played at St. Louis on Saturday, Detroit on Sunday, New York on Thursday, Philadelphia on Saturday and Potts-ville, Pennsylvania, on Sunday. But Nevers missed only 27 minutes of the 1,620 minutes in those 27 games.

"The doctor told me to stay out of one game because of an appendicitis attack," Nevers recalls. "But we were losing and we had to do something.

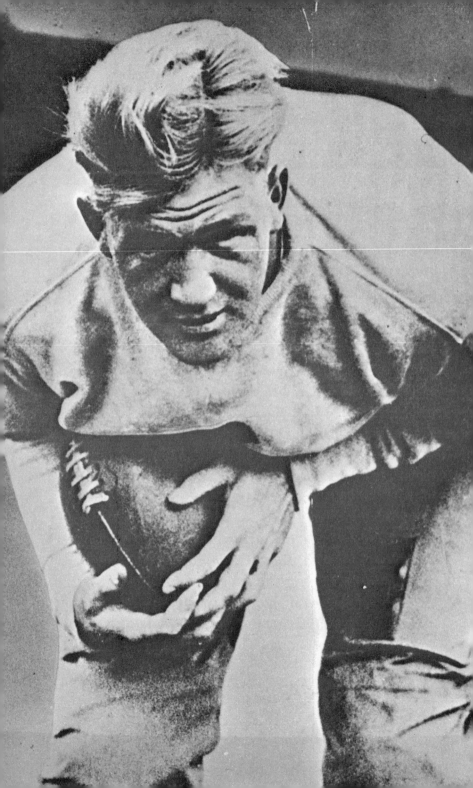

So I went in and threw a 62-yard pass to Joe Rooney." The pass was the longest on record at that time.

In a game at Hartford, Connecticut, Nevers kicked five field goals at distances of 42, 28, 26, 25 and 21 yards. At Pottsville, he completed 17 consecutive passes and scored 27 points. When the Eskimos came to New York to play the Giants, Ernie intercepted a pass on the Duluth 45 and then carried the ball nine straight times to score a touchdown.

At the time of the Giant game the Eskimos had only 15 men on the squad. When Nevers was injured in the fourth period, the Eskimos were hard pressed to put a solid team on the field. Since most of the spectators had come to see Nevers, the Giants agreed to relax the strict rules against substitution then in effect so that Nevers could re-enter the contest before it was over. With New York leading 14-6, and only minutes to go, Ernie came back.

He carried the ball on every play and managed to crash home for a second touchdown just before the final gun. The Giants won 14-13, but not without a bad scare.

Nevers prepares for a game with the Eskimos.

During the 1927 baseball season, Nevers aggravated an old back injury. By the time the football season came, Ernie was in too much pain to play. He sat out the whole football season. When he reported to the St. Louis Browns in the spring of 1928 for his third season in the majors, he was not much improved. The Browns shipped him to the San Francisco Missions of the Pacific Coast League.

Nevers didn't know it, but the Missions had scheduled him to start the day he arrived and had publicized the fact. "My back hurt so bad that it pained me even to lift my arm," he said. "But I didn't want to disappoint the home folks, so I pitched anyhow." He went nine innings and threw a four-hitter but lost 1-0 in his last useful appearance.

Nevers was finished as a baseball pitcher, but he still had his talent for football. The Duluth club was sold in 1929, and Ernie's contract was transferred to the Chicago Cardinals for the 1929 season. His back had improved, and he reported to the Cardinals as playing coach. He led the Cards to a 6-6-1 record and regained his old form as a fullback. The highlight of the season was his

Ernie warms up his pitching arm during his career with baseball's St. Louis Browns.

Nevers is tripped up after a

amazing 40-point performance against the Bears. He remained with the Cards in 1930 and 1931, but was injured again in a postseason exhibition game early in 1932 while leading an all-star team against the Green Bay Packers.

Some pro stars would have been out of the lineup late in an exhibition, but not Ernie. He was the kind of player who insisted on going all out even if the game didn't count. In the final minutes

against the Giants in 1929.

of the game, a Packer lineman fell on his leg and the ankle cracked.

The Cards brought Nevers back to coach again in 1939, but he was fired after a disastrous season in which the Cards won only one game. Except for a brief fling as coach of the Chicago Rockets in the All-America Conference in 1946, he was through with pro sports.

Nevers has settled down at Tiburon, California. If he is pressed for an opinion, Nevers will say that the pros should get away from the T formation and devote more time to a running game. "There ought to be time enough to install a second type of offense beside the T," he has said. "I think they do too much passing now and not enough running, except for Green Bay. That is one reason the Packers are so popular. Nobody knows whether they will run or pass when they come up to the line of scrimmage."

But Nevers has no complaint about the quality of the present-day players.

"They play a little differently these days," he says. "The ball is a little smaller and the equipment is better. But that doesn't mean the players aren't just as tough. A team still has to block and tackle to be good. And the backs still have to cross the goal line to score."

Because accurate statistics were not kept in the early days of the NFL, some of Nevers' accomplishments will not be found in the record books. But he is still the only man in NFL history to score 40 points in one game. He was one of the league's first great fullbacks — and managed a career as a big-time coach and as a professional in two other sports as well.

GALE
SAYERS
chapter
ten

George Halas, who has coached the Chicago
Bears since the National Football League was
organized, was talking about his new rookie Gale
Sayers. Sayers had just scored four touchdowns in
one afternoon against the Minnesota Vikings.
"Red Grange, George McAfee, Gale Sayers —
Gale rates with them all," Halas said.

Halas is not a man who gives compliments
easily. He has seen too many highly rated players
come and go after a season or two in the NFL. So
when he compared Sayers to Grange, football fans
looked again at the young Bear halfback. Before

his first season was over, Sayers had broken two
NFL records and tied another. His rookie year was
the most exciting since that of Grange himself.

Sid Luckman, formerly a great Bear quarterback and now an assistant coach, joined the chorus
of praise. He had played with George McAfee, the
great Bear running back of the 1940s and had
nicknamed McAfee "Gone with the Wind." He
called Sayers "the best back to come into the NFL
since McAfee."

Sayers has the talents of McAfee and some of
his own. He is the most remarkable open-field
runner in the NFL today. He can whirl, spin away,
stop and start without ever losing his balance or
losing sight of his destination. His fakes — slight
movements of his head, shoulders, hips or legs that
seem always to tell what direction he plans to go —
have mystified veteran NFL defensive men. Yet he
is also fast and powerful, sometimes choosing to
run over and away from his defenders instead of
around them.

When Sayers was setting college records at the
University of Kansas, pro scouts dismissed him as
a good prospect for the big leagues. He was no

Bears rookie Gale Sayers waits for game time on the sidelines.

good, they said, because he wouldn't block. But the Bears saw big possibilities for him and were anxious to gain rights to him in the annual college draft. They were afraid that they would miss their chance because the New York Giants had first choice. "We had seen his highlight films, and we wanted him badly," said George Halas later.

The Bears were delighted when the Giants took Tucker Fredrickson, a big, powerful fullback, instead of Sayers. So the Bears got the NFL rights to Sayers, but they still had to worry about his signing with the Kansas City team in the American Football League. They assigned Buddy Young, a former track and football star, to convince Sayers that the NFL and the Bears should be his choice. Buddy must have done a good job because Sayers signed a Bear contract shortly after the NFL draft.

Ironically, even the Bears underestimated their new backfield man. They were hoping to make him a flankerback and use him mostly for pass-receiving chores. It took them a while to realize that Gale is at his best in a position where he can get the ball more directly and run with it. Fortunately, they learned long before his first season was over.

Gale was born in Wichita, Kansas, May 30, 1943, and lived for a time on a farm near the town of Speed, Kansas. He grew up and attended school in Omaha, Nebraska.

Sayers' coach at Omaha Central, Frank Smagacz, disagrees with the pro scouts who said Gale couldn't block. He claims Sayers was the best blocker he ever had. "I don't think the Kansas system was suited to getting the best out of his blocking," said the high school coach. "He always delivered one hundred per cent for us. You know how high school kids are. If one fellow isn't putting out, they let him know."

Smagacz likes to tell this story about a run Sayers made in high school, "One of his best touchdown runs I saw only in the movies. We were playing West Side. They had fourth down and were going for it. Gale, who played both offense and defense for us, was backing up the line on this play.

"They threw a pass that I saw was going to fall incomplete. I turned to the offensive team to tell them to go into the game, but they started laughing. I turned around to see Sayers running for a touchdown after intercepting that pass."

In addition to playing football, Gale became a

track star. He ran the 100-yard dash in 9.7 seconds, and he participated in the high hurdles and the broad jump. But it was his football talent that attracted college scouts from such universities as Notre Dame, Nebraska and Kansas.

His friends in Omaha assumed that Gale would go to the University of Nebraska after graduating from high school. Nebraska was the home-state university and was becoming a football power. But to everyone's surprise, Gale chose Kansas instead.

"I figured Kansas was doing better at the time," said Sayers. "I thought that would give me a better chance to attract the pros. Also, I liked Jack Mitchell, the Kansas coach. I was beginning to think of pro ball as a career, and I wanted to pick the school that I thought would help me most."

As a freshman at Kansas, Sayers scored seven times in two freshman games against Kansas State. In his sophomore year he put on an iron-man show against Oklahoma State and gained 283 yards on 22 carries.

In his junior year (1963), Sayers faced Nebraska, the university of his home state, and set a Big Eight record with a phenomenal 99 2/3-

Sayers skirts two Boston University tacklers and heads for a Kansas touchdown.

yard run. "We had held them at midfield," Sayers recalls. "Their punter kicked out of bounds about one foot short of our goal line. On the first play I took a quick pitchout, took off around end, got a good block from my fullback, fooled the defensive halfback with a change of pace and got in the open."

When he finished his career at Kansas he had scored 20 touchdowns, gained 2,675 yards running and caught 35 passes for 408 yards. He had an amazing average of 6.5 yards per carry.

"He was just great," said Jack Mitchell, his Kansas coach. "Nobody in pro ball is going to catch him. He has great speed, but he doesn't get by on speed alone. He has fine balance and body control and can cut back better than any back I ever saw. The best thing about him was that he always congratulated everybody in the line after he made a touchdown and complimented the blockers who made it all possible."

After his senior season with Kansas, Sayers made several All-America teams and was picked in the first round of the pro draft by the Bears. Late the next summer, he reported to the College All-Stars to play his last game as an amateur before reporting to the Bears' training camp.

The All-Stars practiced at the Bear training field in Rensselaer, Indiana. After only a few plays of the first scrimmage, Sayers limped off the field complaining of a leg injury. Otto Graham, the All-Star coach, was not convinced that the injury was genuine. "This boy Sayers has as great a talent as any athlete I've ever seen," Graham said. "But unless he changes his attitude, he'll never make it with the Bears, because George Halas won't have him."

Although Gale was ready to play by the night of the game, Graham had made other plans, so Sayers saw no action. When he reported to the Bears, Halas used him only sparingly at first, fearing that there might be aftereffects to the injury.

The Los Angeles Rams were the first to get a look at the real Sayers. In an exhibition game at Nashville, Gale ran a punt back 77 yards for one touchdown, scampered 99 yards on a kickoff return and caught a 25-yard touchdown pass.

In the Bear practice sessions, it became obvious that the six-foot, 198-pounder from Omaha was something special. Halas, regrouping his forces for a comeback after a bad season in 1964 (won 5, lost 9), was setting up a wide-open offense. To his delight, Halas discovered that Sayers was adept at running the option play in which the halfback runs wide and has the option of running or passing. Even better, Sayers was a left-handed passer.

Halas took his time with Sayers. Gale sat on the bench most of the time while the Bears were

With Mike Rabold (64) and Jim Cadile (

nning interference, Sayers gains yards for the Bears against Green Bay.

losing to San Francisco and Los Angeles in their first two league games. Halas was saving his rookie for a special job — the game against unbeaten Green Bay.

Although the Bears lost to the Packers 23-14, the game was the turning point of the Chicago season. Sayers, making his first start, scored two touchdowns, one a 65-yard pass play.

Sayers was in the starting lineup to stay. The following week in the return match with the Rams, he shocked the Los Angeles defense by throwing a 26-yard touchdown pass to Dick Gordon. He also went 80 yards with a screen pass from Rudy Bukich, after 300-pound Rosey Grier thought he had flattened him.

"I not only laid a hand on this boy, I thought I ruined him with my shoulder," said Grier. "When I heard the crowd roar, I thought he had fumbled. Instead he was downfield going for the touchdown. That boy is fantastic."

Sayers then attacked the Minnesota Vikings. He scored four touchdowns in a wild and woolly game won by the Bears 45-37. One of his touchdowns came on a spectacular 96-yard kickoff return. When sports writers asked Sayers in the

Leaving Viking defenders behind, Sayers races for the goal line. He scored four touchdowns and gained 324 yards as the Bears won 45-37.

dressing room why he had looked back over his shoulder when he neared the 10-yard line, he said, "I knew I was in the clear. I just wanted to tell my blockers to back off. I didn't want to take a chance on somebody getting called for clipping."

The long kickoff return was the back-breaker for the Vikings who had just taken a 31-30 lead.

"They beat us on the very play we were afraid of," said Coach Norm Van Brocklin of Minnesota. "We tried to kick it out of the park, but the wind held it up and Sayers got it in full stride on his own four. Nobody laid a finger on him."

In the final 15 minutes and 20 seconds of that game in the Vikings' home park, Sayers caught an 18-yard pass and twisted free from two defenders at the 5-yard line to score once, then teamed with Rudy Bukich on another 25-yard touchdown pass. Then he ran 96 yards with the kickoff for his third score and drove through the line from the 10 for the final tally. He had gained an amazing 324 yards on runs, passes, kick runbacks and receptions.

After that big afternoon, they asked Sayers if it was his finest game. "Right now it is," he answered. The season was only half over.

When the Packers came to Chicago for a second look at Sayers, Gale gave them an eyeful. He scored twice on runs of 66 and 10 yards and set up another touchdown with a 62-yard punt return.

"Sayers can be a great one," said Vince Lombardi, the Packer coach. "They didn't beat us with any special plays. The special was Sayers."

Paul Hornung was so impressed that he

commented, "This kid is the greatest to come into the league in my time."

When Sayers put on another spectacular against St. Louis and ran back a kickoff 86 yards before he was caught at the 13, Halas said, "The only reason they caught him was because he was winded. He was all over the field. But I thought his best play was a run up the middle in the fourth quarter. He just refused to be stopped on that one."

New Yorkers got their first look at the new flash when the Bears came to Yankee Stadium in late November for one of their infrequent visits. The 63,000 fans gasped when Sayers lofted a long left-handed pass for a 67-yard gain only to have the play called back because a Bear was holding. The next time the Bears had the ball in a similar situation, Sayers raised his arm in a fake and then took off on a 45-yard touchdown run. He scored twice in a 45-15 romp and gained 185 yards in all categories.

Sayers hit his peak on December 12 when the San Francisco Forty-Niners came to Chicago. By the time the game was over, Sayers had tied the all-time NFL record by scoring six touchdowns. He might have made more if Halas hadn't rested him in the final minutes for fear of injury. Three of the scoring plays measured 85, 80 and 50 yards.

Only two other men have scored six touchdowns in an NFL game, Ernie Nevers in 1929 and

Sayers leaps over Forty-Niner defenders to score one of his six touchdowns on December 12, 1965.

Dub Jones in 1951. Nevers, who scored 40 points against the Bears while playing with the Chicago Cardinals in 1929, saw the game on television in San Francisco.

"I've seen a lot of football, I've seen a lot of

players and a lot of exhibitions, but that was the best performance I've ever seen," said Nevers. "It's a little hard to tell from this distance, but if I'd been coaching, I would have given Sayers another shot at a touchdown."

"He's the greatest runner I've ever seen, and that includes Jim Brown," said Elbert Kimbrough, defensive back of the Forty-Niners.

"The most brilliant exhibition I've ever seen," commented Y. A. Tittle, the great quarterback who is an assistant coach with San Francisco.

When Sayers ended the 1965 season, his first as a pro, he had set an NFL record by scoring 22 touchdowns. Jim Brown, with 21, also topped the old mark of 20 set by Lenny Moore of Baltimore in 1964. The six touchdowns in the Forty-Niner game tied a record, and his total yardage of 336 in that same game set another NFL record. His season total of 2,272 yards gained by runs from scrimmage, kick returns and pass receptions was the third best in the all-time standings.

Sayers has taken his success philosophically. After the season he said, "I didn't think I would do this well in the pros. I just look for a hole and let instinct get me loose." One thing still bothers him, however. "I hate for people to say that I don't block for the other guys," he says.

But for the Bears and their fans, Sayers' blocking seems unimportant as long as he continues to gain the yards and score the points.

INDEX

THE PUNT PASS AND KICK
LIBRARY
N.F.L.